...and all the children said Amen

IAN KNOX

SCRIPTURE UNION
130 CITY ROAD LONDON EC1V 2NJ

For Ruth, Matthew, Jon, Andrew and David.

© Ian Knox 1994

First published 1994

ISBN 0 86201 874 9

Cover design by Mark Carpenter Design Consultants.
Cover illustration and book illustrations by Neil Pinchbeck.

British Library Cataloguing-in-Publication Data
A catalogue record for this book is available from the British Library.

Phototypeset by Intype, London.
Printed and bound in Great Britain by Cox & Wyman Ltd, Reading.

Contents

Preface

They drifted in on a murky afternoon in Minehead. It was optional seminar time at Spring Harvest, and the subject was 'Family prayers'. Each participant at the event had a book of notes, which included a section headed 'For further reading' under each seminar title. But these participants were going to be disappointed, for this particular session had no books to recommend. Instead, their only hope was to buy a cassette of the seminar. There was, apparently, no book on the subject of families praying together. In chatting with my co-presenter of that seminar, Celia Bowring, we agreed I should talk with Scripture Union to see if this lack could be remedied – and this book is here as a result! I am so glad we had that grey day at Butlins in Minehead, and so grateful for the help and encouragement Celia gave me.

The title of this book is from much further back. When I was a boy, we had prayers in our family. With my father and mother, my brothers and sister, I first learned what it meant to pray together. If we had visitors, my dad would enthusiastically end our prayers with, 'And all the people said, Amen.' The adults always seemed amused at this, and we children would smile, not knowing what it meant. Years later I found in my Bible how David had prayed, and that that had been the response to his prayer (1 Chronicles 16:36). My hope and prayer for this book is that families – whoever makes up the 'family' in your home – will be able to pray together, and all the children say, 'Amen.'

Having got the idea and the title for the book, off I went round the country to meet families who prayed together. I cast the net far and wide, both geographically and in the types of family I visited. I went to homes where they had very young children, and others where the children were older or had left. I talked with one-parent families, families where the parents were divorced, families where problems abounded and those families which were very happy. This book is really their book as much as mine, and I am grateful to all who have shared their experiences and given me advice.

Whatever the family's situation, feelings about their prayer life generally fell into four categories. First there were those who said, 'What prayers?'! Then, by far the largest group, was the one where the families *were* praying, but felt dissatisfied with what they were doing. Rather like an entry on a school report, some responded to the question, 'What do you feel about your family prayers?' with the answer, 'Could do better'! One said, 'We are superficial; our prayers don't have the priority they should have.' Another said, 'We are not consistent enough, we lack discipline, and there's too much uncertainty'. After chatting with one dad, he said, 'As a family we're poor at praying, through not putting effort into doing it. I've found this interview difficult and embarrassing.' Another dad described his family prayers as a 'disaster area'. One mum, having made me feel quite inadequate about my own family's efforts, then said of her family, 'We struggle in this; I always wish we could do more.' Most of those who felt dissatisfied with their praying together, agreed with the man who told me, 'We don't do enough. We should be better at it. For all the blessings God gives us, he doesn't get much in return.'

By contrast, some families felt good about what they did. 'Our family prayers are important and necessary,' one couple said. 'People notice a closeness amongst us, and a friendship, which God has given us. We acknowledge his putting us together as a family. We thank God for one another, and our prayers are important to each other. Reality in prayer has kept us open to one another, and we can pray through our relationships.' As I have known that family for many years, I know they are absolutely right – that is the way they are. I heard of another family where their baby's first two words were 'Mummy' and 'Amen' (poor old Daddy!). For one family, their prayers together are 'a life-line', for another 'a must', whilst a third were 'content and relaxed about it'. My favourite comment was from nine year old Simon. I asked him, 'How do you feel about your family's prayers?' and he replied in one word, 'Happy.'

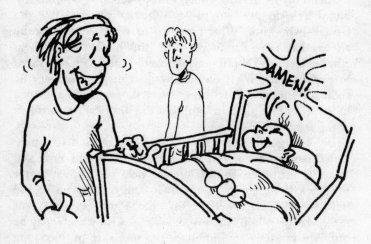

Baby's first two words . . .

I identify most with the families who were not wholly sad or glad about their praying. They said things like:

'Our prayers are probably insufficient – but they're positive when they happen.'

'They go well – but I'm sorry they're not more often,

because they're good.'

'I'm quite happy when we do pray; I feel they're quite successful: but I'd like something more regular and disciplined.'

'We don't do enough – but they're from the heart.'

'They set us up for the day – but there's so much more we should pray for.'

These are a few of the comments which show how most feel – in a dilemma as to how to get our praying right.

Our family does pray together, but nearly everyone I met seems to have a better family prayer life than ours! On the other hand, our prayer times work for us, so I'm not going to spend my life feeling guilty! Our prayers may be ordinary, but there's no need to panic. Whether you feel like the families who said, 'What prayers?'! or whether your family already has a regular prayer time, this book aims to help families feel good about praying together, and to enable them to plan happily. What one family does may or may not be right for another. As in some sweet shops, this is a chance to 'pick 'n' mix', and to work out the practicalities as much as the spiritualities.

I've had good advice from David Spriggs and Christine and Brian Camfield, and lots of help from Maria Prue and Ruth in our office. But my greatest help and inspiration for the book has come from my own family. I happen to live with some brilliant people: my wife, Ruth, and our four sons, Matthew, Jon, Andrew and David. Our prayers may be ordinary, but they are important and special to us. Not long ago I made a video on personal evangelism, which is called *Go for it!* As a result of this book, I pray that each one of us, whatever our home and family situation, will take a look at praying together and 'go for it'.

Ian Knox, May 1994

PART ONE

Big Questions

1

Why bother?

Isn't this book a big fuss about nothing? Don't lots of families get on fine without prayer? Who needs the hassle of arranging the whole thing, of making family prayers actually happen? Is this just one more thing to feel guilty about? Isn't this whole idea of praying together going to be greeted by the family with derision, or, at least, a yawning lack of enthusiasm? Aren't there too many problems to be overcome? Why bother? Is it worth it?

The answer is – yes, it is worth it! And here's why.

Prayer itself

Deep in the heart of almost every person on earth, there is a belief in prayer. This belief may be well hidden, and may only find a means of expression at times of dire need, but it is there.

I once worked with a man who was, by his own admission, an atheist. He was extremely successful in his profession, had a large income and a good family. He felt he had neither the need nor time for God. Then he got a dreadful debilitating disease which left him almost helpless. I met him one day and he began to weep as he told me of his illness. 'Ian,' he said, 'I have no faith in God. But I know you're religious: would you pray for me?'

I prayed with him and continued praying for him on my own for the next couple of weeks till I saw him again. 'I've started praying,' he told me. 'I don't know what to say. I only know the Lord's Prayer, so I say that.' How was it that this atheist began to pray? Why do people in a panic cry out 'Oh God!'? It's simple: because God has placed within each of us a sort of built-in phone line to himself, which we need to use. We need prayer.

Of course, when we do pray, we find that we don't just need to, we want to. We discover the joy of this personal relationship with God. Here is our strength for life and God gives us, in return, the power of his Holy Spirit. Here is the relief of forgiven sins, as the pardon bought by the death of Jesus Christ becomes real in our hearts. Here is hope in despair. For prayer shows us a God who hears and answers.

If we have discovered this to be true, then we can hardly keep it to ourselves. Prayer has become a life-changing experience. How can we fail to share that with the most special people in our lives – our families, those with whom we share our homes? And if our experience of shared prayer is not good so far – boring prayer meetings, dry church services, dull Christians – well, here's a chance to make amends. Our family praying need not be boring, dry or dull. It's up to each of us never to let that happen. Prayer is good, and vital, not just for me alone but for me and the special people around me.

Learning together

Why bother with praying *together*? Because this is a major way in which we discover about God, and ourselves, together. This is how we learn to be Christians. This is how we are able to put God at the centre of our home, and our lives.

What is the writer of Hebrews talking about here?

> And let us consider how we may spur one another on towards love and good deeds. Let us not give up meeting together, as some are in the habit of doing, but let us encourage one another (Hebrews 10:24–25).

Why do we often reserve these verses for churches? Isn't this what Christians are supposed to be doing all the time? Is this what the adults in our homes do with each other? The outside world seems bent on putting us down. Someone has to lift us up. It's hard to be negative about someone we are praying for, especially if they are listening to the prayer! What an encouragement when you hear another member of your family thanking God for you, and asking for God's best in your life.

And what a help it is for children as they grow! Have we forgotten what God told his people thousands of years ago?

> Fix these words of mine in your hearts and minds. . . . Teach them to your children, talking about them when you sit at home and when you walk along the road, when you lie down and when you get up (Deuteronomy 11:18–19).

How will our children learn about God, and about the Bible and prayer, if not from us? Parents are often guilty of expecting others to do their work for them. Anyone else who teaches them – at school, at church, in Sunday groups – is only *in loco parentis*, 'in the place of parents'. All education of children is first the parents' responsibility, with the help of others.

It is to parents that God says:

> Train a child in the way he should go, and when he is old he will not turn from it (Proverbs 22:6).

It's up to us! Paul was able to write to his young friend Timothy:

Continue in what you have learned and have become convinced of, because you know those from whom you learned it, and how from infancy you have known the holy Scriptures, which are able to make you wise for salvation through faith in Christ Jesus (2 Timothy 3:14–15).

And who had taught him 'from infancy'? Why, his gran and his mum!

I have been reminded of your sincere faith, which first lived in your grandmother Lois and in your mother Eunice (2 Timothy 1:5).

Our children learn from us. Our prayers will become their prayers. And, by God's help and through him alone, our faith will become their faith. Don't panic if it takes time. The verse in Proverbs says, 'When he is *old* he will not turn from it.' It does not say 'When he is a teenager'! A child has to

Our children learn from us. Our prayers will become their prayers.

move from a shared faith to one that belongs to him or her personally. If it seems like ages to wait, we must never forget that God loves our children more than we do, and his timing is spot on.

We discover, to our surprise and delight, that the teaching and learning process is not a one-way thing. Children teach us, too. Do we think we can pray? Listen to a small child praying! The younger they are, the better they often pray it seems. Isn't that what Jesus meant when he quoted from Psalm 8?

> From the lips of children and infants you have ordained praise (Matthew 21:16).

A child's mind is not cluttered with life's complications, nor with the doubts adults pick up. He or she has no ghastly religious jargon, either. So there is a trust, an honesty and a directness rarely found in someone older.

That remarkable lady, Dr Helen Roseveare, tells a beautiful story. She was a missionary in the Belgian Congo, before it became Zaire. Shortly after she arrived, she found herself looking after a group of orphans, who treated her as their mother, and with whom she prayed daily. In the maternity ward one day, a mother died in childbirth, leaving a tiny premature baby, as well as a two year old daughter.

Dr Roseveare was desperate to keep the baby warm at night. They used a box for a crib, together with cotton wool and a hot water bottle. The nurse boiled a kettle, filled the bottle and – BANG! – the bottle burst. It was the last one they had. Doctor Roseveare went out to her orphan children, gathered together for lunch, and asked them to pray for the baby, for the nurses to be able to stay awake through the night, and for the baby's sister. Ten year old orphan Ruth started to pray, 'Please God, send a hot water bottle for the baby. And, Oh God, it's no good tomorrow, we need it this afternoon. And we need a dolly for the baby's sister, to show her God loves her.'

I had seen Helen Roseveare talking about this on television. Later she told me how she had been quite unable to say, 'Amen' at the end of Ruth's prayer: she didn't have the nerve to be so direct with God, or to believe God would answer such blunt requests. But that afternoon a truck arrived. Without a word the driver dumped a parcel on the doorstep and drove off. It was the first parcel Dr Roseveare had ever received from England.

Not daring to open it on her own, she called over her orphan family. Out from the parcel came cardigans, bandages and soap. And then there was the unmistakable feel of – yes – a hot water bottle.

'Well,' said Ruth to Dr Roseveare, 'God must have sent a dolly as well. Mummy, can I go with you and give it to the baby's sister to show her God really loves her?' And, without further ado, Ruth reached to the bottom of the parcel and pulled out the doll.

Dr Helen Roseveare writes of her 'family' in one of her brilliant autobiographical books, *Living Faith*, (Hodder) and of how much she learned from those children. My children too, have, on many occasions, reminded me to trust God more, and to expect his love to work. No wonder Jesus himself said:

> I tell you the truth, unless you change and become like little children, you will never enter the kingdom of heaven (Matthew 18:3).

And so, together, parents and children, and whoever makes up your 'family', learn of the wonder of a relationship with God. Together we submit to his authority. The fact that the adults in the home show that they are subject to a higher authority incidentally shows that any authority they exercise comes from God. As we submit to God and his will in prayer, we show how we put ourselves under his care, individually and as a family. It's good to learn together!

Seen and shared

Christians sometimes use the word 'witnessing' in an over-the-top spiritual way. What they mean is sharing their faith with others, by what they say and the way they live. Sometimes practice doesn't quite measure up to the theory.

Praying together as a family is a great way of showing the family's Christian faith and commitment in a natural way. In our home we always say a very short grace before each meal. If someone forgets, another will quickly remind them! Whoever comes, whoever sits at table with us, we say, 'Who's saying grace?' Heads are bowed, grace is said and we get on with the meal.

At birthday parties, whoever's birthday it is says grace. To be honest, we don't make a big thing of it, and, usually, no one ever comments. But after one such birthday, my wife met the mother of one of the young guests at the school gate the next morning. 'You must have had a great party,' said the mum. 'He really enjoyed it . . . He said the best bit of the party was saying grace! In fact, his Dad had got his fork half-way to his mouth at breakfast today, when our son

'You can't eat that, we've not said grace!'

grabbed his hand and said, "You can't eat that, we've not said grace"!!' This poor family, who weren't Christians, were made to say grace by their son for ages afterwards! We had thought very little about saying that grace, but it shook a whole family as a result.

An older friend of one of our sons had long conversations with him about the Christian faith. As a family we never ever talked about anything spiritual with this friend. Again, the only overtly Christian thing to happen was our brief grace before a meal at which he was present, plus the breakfast prayer time when he once stayed overnight. And yet this friend said to our son, 'I hardly have any belief in God at all. But just being in your home almost persuades me to be a Christian.' Believe me, when I think of some of the noise and the arguments he must have heard and seen from time to time, I realise that God's Holy Spirit must have been doing a work of real grace, alongside our 'grace'!

If we have someone staying, we keep up our usual practice of saying grace before meals. We also explain to them in advance that we have a family prayer time at breakfast each day. If they want to avoid it, we give them every opportunity of doing so, especially if they are not Christians, or would feel embarrassed. We still give them breakfast though! We find, almost without exception, that visitors, whatever their own beliefs, are more than pleased to share our prayer time with us. Christians who do not have such a time in their own home, seem to find it extra special. Perhaps they will go home and give it a try!

Praying in this way is a witness *to* others, but it can also be a witness *with* others. I know some of our close relations pray for our family when they meet as a family, and in so doing stand with us in the work we do in evangelism, spreading the good news of Jesus Christ.

This witnessing together is a source of strength and encouragement, and works sometimes in particularly wonderful ways. A close friend was telling me how, after her mother died, she had had a very bad time. One night, unable

17

to sleep, she had cried out, 'Oh God, I can't cope.' Almost at once she had fallen asleep, and slept soundly till ten the next morning. Three or four days later she received a letter from a lady whom she had met at a conference. She related in the letter how she had felt prompted to pray for my friend, though she did not know why. It was at the exact moment my friend had cried out. Our witnessing together in prayer is a lifeline of hope and love.

Togetherness

It's a corny old saying, 'The family that prays together, stays together.' But that's what they say! And in these days, anything which may hold families together is worth a try. In the western world we are in serious danger of seeing family life disintegrate. In the last twenty-five years, the divorce rate in Britain has risen from one marriage in six to more than one marriage in three. In most predictions, the year 2010 is the time when divorces will equal weddings, as happens in the United States today.

Eighty per cent of families never meet together.

And yet, in recent surveys, when people were asked, 'What is the most important thing in life?' top of the poll came 'Family'. The very thing we want is the thing most under threat. I could hardly believe another recent statistic: eighty per cent of families never meet together. What about meal-times? Surely families sit down together then? No, we have microwaves, so food is simply put on plates, and when you want to eat you pick up your plate and pop it in for three minutes. Sadly, today, people's lives are often so hectic, responsibilities and needs so varied, that it can be almost impossible for a family to find a time to eat together. In our home we aim to eat together (as often as possible), laugh together, cry together – and *pray* together.

By so doing, we try to give to each other the love and encouragement and support which comes from our hearts, and from God's heart, too. I count it a privilege to respond positively to the request, 'Please pray for me' from our eldest son, who has now left home. He knows he is not alone when we are able to assure him in our letters, 'We prayed for you this morning.'

This togetherness in prayer becomes a natural part of daily life. Our youngest son has a habit, on the dullest and wettest of days, of praying, 'Thank you, Lord, for these lovely days you've given us.' He means it! I open my eyes, look out of the window as he prays this, and smile. But he is doing what Paul says:

> Always giving thanks to God the Father for everything (Ephesians 5:20).

And he probably doesn't even know Paul said it! When one of our rugby playing sons asks God for a good game, and not to get injured, or we pray for the flute lesson, or the school assembly, we are also doing what the Bible tells us:

> In everything, by prayer and petition, with thanks-giving, present your requests to God (Philippians 4:6).

The effect on the everyday life of the family member is enormous. After all, your boring old French test got prayed about! And in times of crisis, you remember that prayer together is the answer. I discovered this most powerfully at three o'clock one morning. One of our sons, then aged three, was having disturbed nights. On this particular night I was awakened by his cries. Groping half-awake into his room, I found him shouting, 'It's the wolves, it's the wolves!' I'm not at my best at 3am. This is my excuse for what happened next. 'Don't panic,' I said, 'I'll chase them away.' I didn't know what the wolves were – a bad dream probably. I opened the window, and ordered, 'O.K. you wolves. Out you go – shoo, shoo.' Then I closed the window, and gave my son a quick kiss. 'It's all right now, I've sent them away, so let's get back to sleep.'

Rather pleased with myself, I moved towards the door. 'Daddy,' the little voice called, 'You've not asked Jesus to look after me.' There are moments in your life when you are glad no one can see you! I had felt so clever, but had forgotten the only thing that really mattered. Very chastened, I went back to the bed, held my son tightly in my arms, and prayed with him. Before I had finished praying he was soundly asleep; his fears had found their true answer. Incidentally, we have found that when a child prays himself, we often discover his previously unspoken fears as he brings them to God, and so can help him to overcome them.

Impact

This consistent praying together makes an impact on my whole attitude and approach to life. It becomes normal to be a Christian! It sharpens my reactions to right and wrong.

A little while ago, we opened a packet of breakfast cereal to discover a small plastic figure, of the sort you might find as a giveaway from the cereal companies, but this one was different. It was grotesque, and everything about it seemed evil. Instead of giving it to one of the children, I sent it back to the company. In my letter I quoted from Philippians:

> Whatever is true, whatever is noble, whatever is right, whatever is pure, whatever is lovely, whatever is admirable – if anything is excellent or praiseworthy – think about such things (Philippians 4:8).

I asked the company if this little model fulfilled any of these words, and why my children were having to start the day looking at something evil. To my delight, and much to the credit of the company concerned, I received a very genuine letter of apology, and an assurance that future promotions would not repeat this wrong. Our breakfast praying may not change the world, but an occasional nudging in the right direction must be good!

Why do we bother to pray together? For all the reasons I've given. But it was perhaps best put in John Bunyan's *Pilgrim's Progress*. The hero of that book is a man called Christian. On his journey from the City of Destruction to the Celestial City he climbs up a hill to the Palace Beautiful. When he arrives he asks the Porter, 'Sir, what house is this?' The Porter replies, 'This house was built by the Lord of the hill, and he built it for the relief and security of pilgrims.'

That's how we want our home to be. For those who live in our home, and for those who visit, we want 'the Lord of the hill' to make it his home, too. As we join with him in prayer together, he does just that. When I was a boy growing up in Yorkshire, my father led us in prayer each day. Very often he would pray, 'May this be a home of peace and love, where the Lord Jesus is to be found.' Through the poor response of one or two (well, me actually!) it didn't always seem that way, but it set a goal, and by and large I do remember the 'peace and love'.

Now my wife, Ruth, and I have our home. We want to make Dad's prayer ours. And – whoever makes up the 'family' who lives together in your home – God wants that for you too, as the next chapter will show.

2

Who says so?

Prayer is God's idea! If, in our home, we want to pray together, then we will be doing what he wants. A few minutes flicking through a Bible will show this is true.

A stroll through the Old Testament

Togetherness, marriage, families: they are all within God's creation plan for us. He said:

> It is not good for the man to be alone (Genesis 2:18).

> A man will leave his father and mother and be united to his wife (Genesis 2:24).

> He [God] blessed them and said to them, 'Be fruitful and increase in number' (Genesis 1:28).

We have his blessing on our marriages, families and homes. More than that, he wants us to know him, and his love, within our homes. I quoted from Deuteronomy 11 in the last chapter, and it is significant that those verses repeat what God had already said earlier. In chapter 6 he refers to his greatest commandment of all, in verse 5, and then goes on to speak of all the commandments in verse 7:

> Love the Lord your God with all your heart and with all your soul and with all your strength ... Impress [these commandments] on your children. Talk about them when you sit at home and when you walk along the road, when you lie down and when you get up ... Write them on the door-frames of your houses (Deuteronomy 6:5, 7, 9).

This is a lot more than hearing God's word in church. This is the adults in every home sharing it with those under their own roof. There can be no more powerful example to children than when they hear and see their older family members sharing in prayer and the study of the Bible.

As we move into the Psalms, we find plenty of encouragement from God to be a family which prays together.

> Sons are a heritage from the Lord, children a reward from him (Psalm 127:3).

If this is so, it seems crazy to try to raise those children without any reference to the God who gave them to us.

And some serious involvement with God in our homes might be a real benefit to us if David is right when he says:

> I was young and now I am old, yet I have never seen the righteous forsaken or their children begging bread (Psalm 37:25).

Throughout our lives, God longs to help us. One of my sons was troubled recently as he faced a series of major exams. As he was away, I wrote to him these words from Proverbs:

> Trust in the Lord with all your heart and lean not on your own understanding; in all your ways acknowledge him, and he will make your paths straight (Proverbs 3:5–6).

I was glad that I could assure him of our prayers as a family and of God's love at the moment of need. For me, as I said in the last chapter, it is a part of doing as God tells me:

> Train a child in the way he should go, and when he is old he will not turn from it (Proverbs 22:6).

For God's part, he longs to:

> . . . open the floodgates of heaven and pour out so much blessing that you will not have enough room for it (Malachi 3:10).

They did it!

Some families look back to Old Testament times and draw inspiration for their homes from the way the Jewish people lived long ago (indeed, many still live this way today). The traditions they built up of being together, of sharing meals as whole families, of believing in a special covenant relationship with God, are ones which deserve our consideration, and even our initiation. They really believed God was among his people, even as they ate together.

One lady shared with me that her inspiration came from the example of Hannah, in 1 Samuel 1, who wanted a child, and then gave him to the Lord. In a similar way this twentieth century lady was able to hand over her children to God. Perhaps it was because of his mother's example that Samuel, when he had grown up, said to the people:

> As for me, far be it from me that I should sin against the Lord by failing to pray for you (1 Samuel 12:23).

What a spur for our prayers for those we love!

Not only are Bible characters an example for us, we can see them as models for our children to copy too. The great men and women of God were people of prayer. Psalm 90 has the heading: 'A prayer of Moses the man of God'. Moses knew how very much he needed God's help, as he led the Israelites from Egypt, and so he prayed. Abraham prayed for his family, in danger of being destroyed in the evil cities of Sodom and Gomorrah (Genesis 18), and so we can pray for the protection of those we care about. Daniel was one of the greatest men of God, and is famous for praying daily – even at the cost of being thrown to the lions (Daniel 6). Deborah sang praises to God (Judges 5), as did Miriam (Exodus 15).

Whatever else we want for our children, surely most of all we long for them to be God's men and women. So we must help them to grow as those who pray and, like those heroes of old, walk closely with God.

Jesus said . . .

Far from saying, 'Oh well, all this praying was a good idea up till now, but as I'm here you don't need it any more', Jesus made it clear by his teaching and his example that his disciples should pray.

He wants us to pray. He told his disciples to '. . . always pray and not give up' (Luke 18:1). In introducing what we now call 'The Lord's Prayer', or 'The Family Prayer' in Matthew 6, Jesus did not say, 'If you pray' but 'When you pray'. It's something he expects to happen. The prayer itself shows how much God wants to be involved in our everyday lives, as 'our father', the ultimate head of our families. He cares about the very bread we eat, and forgives us our sins, giving us his power to protect us from evil. The importance of acknowledging his holiness and his glory is there also.

Jesus makes great promises to us if we do pray:

> If you believe, you will receive whatever you ask for in prayer (Matthew 21:22).

25

> Whatever you ask for in prayer, believe that you have received it, and it will be yours (Mark 11:24).

Even if we struggle with these verses sometimes, I find it terrific to realise that as our family prays together at breakfast, Jesus has promised:

> Where two or three come together in my name, there I am with them (Matthew 18:20).

With such an assurance, who wouldn't want to pray!

I'm not a great one for 'negatives', but I am aware that not to help my family in their relationship with God will work to their disadvantage. I may shrug my shoulders with a 'So what?' but God views things more seriously, and Jesus puts it in the strongest possible language:

> Things that cause people to sin are bound to come, but woe to that person through whom they come. It would be better for him to be thrown into the sea with a millstone tied round his neck than for him to cause one of these little ones to sin (Luke 17:1–2).

That's strong talk! I would rather err on the side of caution, because, as Jesus said:

> Your Father in heaven is not willing that any of these little ones should be lost (Matthew 18:14).

He is concerned for their (and our) well-being. In that beautiful part of the Sermon on the Mount beginning at Matthew 6:25, Jesus explains how our heavenly Father knows how we need food and clothing, and cares enough to supply them. We live in a society and a culture which follows a creed of people helping themselves, instead of, 'Ask and it will be given to you' (Matthew 7:7). We have to let God turn our thinking to his way, and help our children to realise the love Jesus has for us all. In our praying together, they will discover with us that Jesus' promises come true.

And if things do go wrong, then what can we do but pray? So much of Jesus' teaching makes us realise our praying is not wasted. His great parable of the prodigal son in Luke 15 has often been a lifeline for parents of wayward children who have grown up and gone away from them and God. And when the family has its rows we can ask Jesus to make true for us his own prayer in John 17:22 '. . . that they may be one.'

The words of Jesus urge us to pray. But his example is equally potent . . .

He did it!

Jesus prayed. Indeed, he shames our poor prayer lives, when we read things like:

> Very early in the morning, while it was still dark, Jesus got up, left the house and went off to a solitary place, where he prayed (Mark 1:35).

Can you imagine any situation where Jesus needed to pray, and we don't?! When a small boy gave him a few poor loaves and a couple of fish, did Jesus look down his nose and say they wouldn't make much of a meal? He did the opposite, and 'gave thanks' to God (John 6:11). Not many of us today say a grace when it's only a snack, but I expect this boy's family prayed every time they ate together after that!

We will search long and hard to find a greater encouragement to involve Jesus in our families than the incident in Mark when he welcomed parents and their children, though others seemed to find them a nuisance. As the disciples tried to push them away, Jesus said:

> 'Let the little children come to me, and do not hinder them, for the kingdom of God belongs to such as these.

27

I tell you the truth, anyone who will not receive the kingdom of God like a little child will never enter it.' And he took the children in his arms, put his hands on them and blessed them (Mark 10:14–16).

I thank God that his Son welcomes children, and his actions then enthuse me to bring my children to him now for his blessing. And when, in my own and my family's life, all seems hopeless, I remember Jesus kneeling in the Garden of Gethsemane, and pouring out his heart to God. His regret was the failure of his 'family' of close disciples to pray also (Matthew 26:40). It is good to follow his example, and to bring our deepest hurts and needs to a loving Father. Right up to his return to heaven, Jesus loved to pray with this 'family'. The two at Emmaus recognised him in their home when he 'gave thanks' (Luke 24:30). Jesus is our great example in praying.

And so on . . .

With such a hero, the early Christians couldn't do anything else but follow suit. The New Testament is a constant encouragement for our family prayers. 'Pray continually' (1 Thessalonians 5:17) and 'Pray in the Spirit on all occasions' (Ephesians 6:18), mean more than an occasional church visit. To 'give thanks in all circumstances' (1 Thessalonians 5:18) sounds as if it needs doing on most days, whatever the situation at home. Which is exactly what the first Christians did:

They broke bread in their homes and ate together with glad and sincere hearts, praising God (Acts 2:46–47).

If that's how it started, shouldn't we keep going in the same way?

Throughout the epistles there is not so much a sense of 'you must', but more the feeling of 'look at the benefits of sharing our lives with each other, and with God, as we pray'. So we 'carry each other's burdens, and in this way . . . fulfil the law of Christ' (Galatians 6:2), which at least one of my friends says is the first and main reason her family prays together. Getting rid of wrongs, our very well-being, is tied up with prayer:

> Confess your sins to each other and pray for each other so that you may be healed (James 5:16).

I find that Paul's teaching about the body of Christ, in 1 Corinthians 12, has a genuine outworking in our family, where we need each other's Christian contributions to make us a complete family body.

Best of all, every family ought to discover the splendour and comfort of these two verses:

> Do not be anxious about anything, but in everything, by prayer and petition, with thanksgiving, present your requests to God. And the peace of God, which transcends all understanding, will guard your hearts and your minds in Christ Jesus (Philippians 4:6–7).

3

Who's in on this?

Two boys were praying. 'God, if you're real, please touch me,' prayed the first. There was silence, till the second boy said quietly, 'God, if you want a hand, you can use mine.'

I don't care if someone made it up, it's a good story! God does touch lives, and he often does it through people. If we want him to touch our families, we must let him work through us. We must be the ones who help the spiritual life at home to work. The initiative is with us: as President Truman had on his desk at the White House, 'The buck stops here'. Praying together is for *me* to make happen. Or is it?

Who leads?

In the Victorian household, the father would be character-ised as sitting in state with the large family Bible in his hands, glasses on the end of his nose, adoring and silent children around him, and his wife submitting to his supreme authority as the head and leader of this holy time! Each person knew their place, and he accepted his duty and responsibility to read and pray with and for the family each day.

Whilst few would want to go back to this style, the different family structures of the present time − one-parent families, two busy parents both in full-time employment, etc

– can create a situation of no leadership, with no one feeling responsible for the family's prayer life. Who should take the lead in this? The simple answer is, it doesn't matter, as long as someone does!

In speaking with many families about this question, I realised it came down to two things – opportunity and motivation. Opportunity means that whoever is there takes the lead. So, 'When my wife is there, she takes the lead,' or 'I go off to work early, but my husband always prays with the children before they go to school.' Another reaction would be 'I take the lead to get it going,' And I appreciated the honesty of the man who said, 'I do, but my wife prompts me!'

The greater part of leadership is in motivation, and the more the whole family gets into praying together, the more anyone can be the initiator of the family's prayers on any specific day. In our home, it is often the person in the greatest rush who makes things happen. One of the children might say, 'I've got to see a teacher, can we pray *now*?' Several families I spoke with have child-led prayer times. 'The children remind us,' I was told by one couple. Another reply was, 'Our six year old son.' A mum said, 'Me, my husband, or our elder daughter.' These were typical answers to the question 'Who leads?' One man admitted it was 'usually someone else'!

If, for some reason, one person finds it very difficult to give a lead, don't let this become an uncomfortable pressure on them. In one Christian home I know well, it is the mum who invariably makes family prayers happen, because her husband cannot forget his childhood horror story. His dominant father imposed God on his family: each day there would be a reading from a devotional book and one from the Authorised Version of the Bible, adult notes of explanation, the mention of numerous missionaries, and prayers to open and close, all done by Father. My friend describes each such daily occasion as boring, impersonal and lifeless. He has been so hurt by all this, that he is now afraid his own children will experience the same feelings of revulsion. So his wife, without these hang-ups, leads their family prayers. She understands his predicament, but does not let it stop the family praying together.

Who takes part?

In our home, everyone gets in on the praying, although usually my wife, Ruth, or I do the Bible reading. Only one person prays aloud each day, but everyone is given the opportunity to do this in a fairly random way. Whoever is leading will usually ask someone to pray, unless there is a quick volunteer. In some homes, it is always Mum or Dad who prays, but we have found it a help and a blessing, for both child and parent alike, if the praying is shared by everyone.

I'm going to deal with 'What if someone doesn't want to?' later in the book. In one family where all are encouraged to pray, Mum said that those who pray are: 'My husband, me, our daughter always, and the boys – sometimes!' Most homes seem not to have any set rules as to 'who does what'. The initiator may also be the enthusiast for the praying. If a child says, 'Let's do it,' they may be willing to pray out loud for the family on that occasion, so seize the moment and build on their enthusiasm, encouraging their faith and confidence.

When all else fails, our family falls back on Mum or Dad although it's great when, in answer to a request to pray, a voice pipes up, 'I will.' The main thing is to be *relaxed* about it. I loved the way one mum told me: 'We are fairly chaotic. Sometimes it works wonderfully and everyone contributes. Other times I think, "Ah well, tomorrow's another day".'

An evolving role

Taking part may take time. Parents will have to work out when babies turning into toddlers can first get in on the action. The first prayer by a young child is often treasured and remembered as a special moment. Years later, a smile will still come with the memory of that two year old starter: 'Ankoo God for Granny and Grandpa and Fido. Please bless Fido.' This really was the first prayer of one child I know, because his mother told me (I've changed the dog's name to protect the real animal). Where were the parents in the prayer? And why did the dog alone get a blessing? But Mum was proud of this great first effort!

We have always wanted to include each child in our family praying from as soon as they felt able to join in. Some quiet prompting has sometimes helped, though there has also, quite rightly, been the rejoinder, 'I can do it myself!' As one father told me about his small daughter, 'She's caught it. She's got into it.' When the family prays, each new member should naturally filter in, as they grow.

In one family I know, they began to pray together when the eldest son was small, and had just learned to write. The first thing he wrote out were his prayers, which he then read at prayer time. The next son, unable to write, dictated his prayers to his older brother, who then read them out! Since then these boys have moved on from five and three, and pray without notes!

We need to remember, in the evolving role of children, that they are not all going to respond in the same way. One family has a son who, from an early age, was aware of problems in his life, and was glad to bring God into all his needs. His parents wrongly assumed his younger sister would be the same, and struggled with her self-assurance. She not only did not feel a need to pray, she would even hide the family's *Daily Light*, from which they read every morning, and a game of hide-and-seek had to take place to find it each day! But, when they played her little game, she was then willing to join in.

In a similar way, one child will be self-conscious, while another will be difficult to keep quiet. One will pray off the cuff, while a second will enjoy set prayers, a collect, or

She hid their Daily Light.

the Lord's Prayer. Some lack self-confidence, and a book of children's prayers for them to read from can help. For some children, a sense of knowing God personally may be the key, as they feel God does want to listen to them, and cares enough to be involved in their lives.

This evolving style can, ultimately, go either way. Some parents have told me how their family prayers have faded away. 'It's not so workable now they're older,' one will say. Another commented, 'They got more self-conscious by ten or eleven.' And one person said with sadness, 'Life got more disorganised, and we lost our daily discipline.' Sometimes there is real rebellion. 'Gradually things went wrong at church. Now our eldest daughter doesn't want to know,' a mum told me. 'In our family time she took part less and less. In the end she would sit with her arms folded, showing us that she did not want to join in.' Each family has to decide what is right for them. And this will probably change at the different stages of the family's life together.

Occasionally, it might be right to make a deliberate decision *not* to pray together, for the best of motives. In one clergy family I know well, the family stopped praying together when the children were about eleven years old. The parents knew that each child was being encouraged in their spiritual growth through their own peer groups at church. They knew that the children prayed themselves, and so they consciously held back to allow them to develop on their own. Now their children are grown up, all are Christians, so their parents' decision has proved right. But one daughter has recently remonstrated with them for the lack of family prayers during her teens!

On the other hand, the evolution of children's involvement can progress further and further forward. In one family, the mother fell seriously ill while her husband was abroad. Rushed into hospital, she left her two teenage children to fend for themselves. After a couple of days, she urged the children to pray for Dad. 'Oh, we have been,' they said, and related how the family prayer time had carried on 'as usual' in the absence of both parents!

For our family, I guess we are somewhere in a middle course between these two positions. We live on a plateau. We are beyond the baby stage, and have levelled out to a regular routine which, whilst not going backwards, now makes no great progress. That sounds rather unsatisfactory, but it isn't. We have all grown to a point where we can share in a meaningful way in prayer, and it feels good.

Involving others

While a child naturally comes into the family circle, and joins in automatically, what should happen about visitors, be they relatives or friends, Christians or not? There are several choices, and each home must make a decision with which its members are comfortable.

Some tell me, frankly, that anyone outside the family does not join their family prayers, or would only do so in exceptional circumstances. At the other extreme, others would treat visitors as if they were family, and make sure they felt as important as if they were, very much including them in family prayers. Most would find a point somewhere in between, and struggle a little to get a right balance.

Starting from the 'exclusion' zone, some would be willing to include close relatives, as long as they were Christians. Or it might be right to include non-relatives who were Christians. One solution is to have a simple prayer with a visitor, and to have a separate family time when the visitor is not around. A single friend of mine has a system where he will pray with people who come, but not as part of his regular 'family' prayers. Those in the house will pray with the visitors about the issues raised in their conversation, but they will not be invited to the family time – prayers with visitors are extras.

I know one lovely home where the children's Christian school friends will call in time to join in with the family's prayers at breakfast time en route for the rigours of the classroom! If a visitor is staying overnight, they need to be told that there will be a prayer at breakfast, enabling them to delay coming down in the morning if they wish to, but with an easy-going invitation to join the prayer time if they want. If they stay for more than a few days, they will probably get involved sooner or later.

Some families use their prayers as a witness to others. Often grace before meals is said whoever is present. This needs to be done with sensitivity to the visitor, but without any feeling of embarrassment on the family's part. A relaxation of the norm might be allowed: if, for example, a family usually held hands to say grace, they might not do this if guests or family members would be embarrassed. Similarly, some families said that their teenagers sometimes ask that grace is *not* said when certain friends are present. Loving sensitivity towards one another is important as we help each other grow in our Christian faith.

Interestingly it is usually the family who feel the pressure, not the visitor. Those homes which entertain members of other faiths will not find their grace objected to, especially if it gives thanks to God for the visitors, and asks God to be present at the meal. One close friend of mine will choose his words carefully if a visitor of another faith is present, such as, 'Lord, for all your mercies and this food make us truly grateful.' By not mentioning Jesus specifically, he avoids unnecessary offence. He cannot have family prayers with such a visitor, but he will always pray.

So we progress to the total involvement of the visitor. One father told me: 'We naturally include them. They take part just because they are here. We never suggest they should or shouldn't. If they are down to breakfast, they join us for prayer.' Children can be a great help in making the outsider feel at home in prayer. One mum has non-Christian parents, but her children tell them, 'We have to talk to Jesus,' and involve their grandparents in a way Mum cannot. Some single folk might especially appreciate being allowed to share. One couple I know let their single friends put their small daughter to bed, and they are happy to pray with her as part of her bedtime routine. Sharing her prayer time increases their sense of being 'family'.

In our home, our style would be to involve any visitor in grace, which we say at every meal. At our breakfast time reading and praying, a visitor would automatically be brought in if they were there. If they were a Christian, we might well ask them to pray for us. We would probably not share anything too intimate that day, to avoid embarrassment all round.

In the end, who shares and who prays is a decision for those who make up the family. From time to time that decision may need to be varied or reviewed. Even when the participants are known, the 'What shall we do?' questions still have to be worked out – so let's look at those next.

4

What's to do?

What do families *do*, when they pray together? What actually happens? My favourite answer came from a friend who said, 'Not a lot!' The more people I asked, the more that answer was repeated. Activity in most family prayer times *is* limited, and the ideas in this chapter are ideals. No one family does everything. Most do very little.

If you have decided you want to do more, an extension of grace at mealtimes may be a good starting point for a daily family prayer time. One family who has done this, told me that any meal will do, and the praying varies according to particular needs, the chaos prevailing, and the ability of the youngest to sit still! If a family is very busy, even a daily extended grace may not be possible and, even if it is, a brief thanks for the meal may be all that happens. We live in a madly over-active world, and many of us need to look seriously at our lifestyles.

Assuming we want to look at serious and realistic possibilities, this whole question needs to be worked out, and worked at. Some families see family prayers as the family praying together and no more. For example, on occasion someone might say, 'I think we should just thank God for that,' or 'Could you pray for me? I'm so scared about going to the dentist', and the family, by responding practically, brings prayer into ordinary day-to-day life.

Most families who pray together, whether regularly or occasionally, seem to concentrate on specific concerns. It is good to pray as and when things come up, especially if they are not always concerned with great crises. Where a church has a 'prayer circle', a family may pause to pray for the need which has been phoned through, or give thanks when all is well. Our daily praying at home, on the whole, majors on the needs of that day. We ask each person what he or she is doing and pray for God's help for them. In many families the members know each other so well that there is no need even to check the agenda.

One good thing about this style is that it does enable the family to talk happily and seriously over how things are, and to work through issues, knowing that God is also going to be involved in their joys, sorrows, hopes and fears. There is the chance to express thanksgiving, and to look out beyond the immediate circle to the wider family, and the world. Even the morning paper can highlight a major concern. This simple praying, which is unlikely to be heavy, can be a great blessing.

A step forward is to include a reading as well. Our family, like many others, often reads a few verses from the Bible in our prayer time. If a reading doesn't seem to work, it can be dropped for a while. Another style would be to extend the praying from just one person praying aloud for the family's needs to several taking part in this way. One family told me how they sit in a circle on the floor and pray around it, taking turns. Sometimes they talk about what to pray for as they go round the circle. A family with slightly older children told me how sometimes an evening meal would flow naturally into 'communion' whenever that felt right, using a roll and Ribena.

Another family astonished me with their answer to the question, 'What do you do in your prayer time?' They begin each day with grace at breakfast, followed by prayers for the day. Two or three times a week they go round the family in prayer, arguing as to who should start because they are all so enthusiastic. Sometimes they read from a Christian book, or use prayers from a prayer book, and they learn Bible verses together. Each Friday night they sit in the lounge, light a candle, put a cross on the table, and pray round the circle, including the Lord's Prayer, also occasionally reading a couple of verses from the Bible. Before Sunday lunch, they worship. Inspired by Jewish family life, they light a candle, asking the question, 'Why do we light a candle?' and answering, 'Because Jesus is the light of the world.' This is followed by, 'Why do we do this on a Sunday?' Answer: 'Because Jesus rose from the dead on Sunday.' Question: 'Who is Jesus?' Answer: 'The King of Kings.' Then comes grace, and their meal.

Reading and singing

Many people include some sort of reading, in addition to prayer. Diving into the Bible sometimes, if not every day, will help prayers along, and inspire and encourage daily Christian living.

One of my relatives was very excited by his family's daily readings from Luke's Gospel, which they worked through a few verses at a time. They also tried Revelation, up to chapter seven. When they didn't know what to read, someone would turn to Proverbs and simply stab a finger at any verse, which they would then talk about. Maybe you have some misgivings about this latter approach! However, the habit of taking a verse or two is a good one. The Good News Bible is particularly helpful, especially as it is divided into short, headed paragraphs, one of which is enough for each day.

Some find the Bible especially helpful at festivals, such as Harvest and Easter, or on other special occasions. A number of homes get help from daily Bible notes from organisations like Scripture Union (*Find out about . . . , Quest, One to One, Alive to God*) or CWR (*Every Day with Jesus, Topz*). One friend says she and her family have worked through *The Lion Children's Bible* three times, and they also love *The Lion Book* of *Children's Prayers*. Younger children enjoy *Little Fish Books* (Scripture Union). One family with older children has followed *Living Light* (Kingsway), gone *Through the year with Watchman Nee*, and is currently using *Day by Day* by Wong Ming-Dao (Highland).

We have never used any notes or other books, preferring to save these for our individual quiet times. Over the years we have gone through each Gospel, most of the Psalms, quite a lot of the epistles, and Acts. It is amazing how much you can read when each day has a few verses. If it is appropriate, a one sentence 'thought for the day' from the reading by one of us leads into our prayer.

There are some families (but not many) who sing as well. Perhaps because all our children are boys, we don't tend to, though we do sing grace if we have visitors. If there is a musician in your family, you may feel quite enthusiastic about singing. Praise tapes go well in some homes. Every family has its own favourites. Lots of children enjoy ones by Ishmael. I think singing works best with smaller children. Songs picked up at a Christian holiday, or at church and Sunday groups can be for sharing around the house, or in the car. Getting a new tape for a holiday trip will for ever associate those songs with that time. Songs are a good way for children to be able to teach their parents, rather than the more usual way around. It can be sad when singing days fade away in the awkwardness of growing up.

What prayer?

What does a family pray about when it is together? It's amazing what people say. One person told me, 'We pray about important things in the family – exams, driving tests, and washing machines that burst into flames.' I was left wondering how often they had resat driving tests, and what kind of washing machine they had! But that is what most prayers are made up of – the immediate needs of family members. We tend to be responsive to the events of yes-

We pray about important things . . .

terday, today and tomorrow, and how life affects us. Troubles and concerns dominate. One family prayed for the son whose friends played games he disliked, leaving him no one to be with. (They changed the game the next day, I was told!)

As we pray like this, we learn of God's love for us in all circumstances. One boy could not get his work done in time, so the family prayed that he would not resent finishing his work last. He came home the following day to say that he had prayed about the problem whilst in the classroom. What a valuable lesson to learn that God was right there with him! The younger someone is when they discover God's concern for the ordinary details of their life, the closer will be their relationship with him as they grow. A friend's small son prays every day for his favourite dog, much to the delight of his older sisters, heightened by the express speed with which he prays, allegedly getting three sentences into one eighth of a second!

In our home we are glad to pray for the normal events of each day – the music lesson, PE, swimming and games, a meeting or a journey, as well as a major exam, or a vital interview. There will almost certainly be a concern for our immediate world, too, especially if a relative or close friend is ill. When a neighbour is bereaved, he or she will be remembered. Many a home will bring crises in the national and international news to God, especially ones to which we can relate, such as war and famine. Church needs are close to many hearts, such as the one I heard of from a friend. He received a letter from the Missionary Aviation Fellowship, asking him to find a field near his home for an airstrip for a training flight. He got his young family to pray that God would find such a field, especially as 'God can see'. Within a day or so a farmer offered four or five strips, and the children learned that God had the answer, even though they didn't.

The other strength of this 'asking' style of praying together is that it enables different family members to express what is important to them personally. One girl I know always prays for her sick gran, pregnant women and babies! Equally, the asking can lead naturally to thanks and praise. We try, in our prayers, always to include gratitude, if only for the new day. Thanksgiving is a way of making life positive, and can become a major feature of the family's life. In turn, it can lead to worship, which is quite hard in a small group of people who know each other so well.

It is in the home where we can be at our worst, too. There needs to be room for saying 'sorry', and prayer gives the double opportunity to own up to God and to each other, especially if, as a friend put it to me, there has been a 'heavy day'. One little girl I know asks each day for her sin to be taken away, and for the Holy Spirit to fill her life – not a bad prayer for all the family to add their 'Amen' to. When we, in our home, have a 'heavy day', Ruth, my wife, will be the one who asks God for his help for us all to act more lovingly, letting him take away our unkindness. By so doing, we can receive God's help to forgive each other too, and even to give that reassuring hug – surely a picture of the way God deals with us as well.

So prayer means praying about anything and everything relevant to our everyday lives. Each person then learns to involve God in their moment-by-moment living. A friend was delighted when his twelve year old said, 'I'm not going to pray just to win at football, I'm going to pray for others too. I don't just want to butter God up!'

Real prayer

I believe one of the finest ways to learn the secret of real prayer is to pray together as a family. Together we can discover God's Holy Spirit leading us, inspiring us and guiding us into the closest possible relationship with the Father, through our Lord Jesus Christ. The children may well give the lead, as they instinctively trust God without the hang-ups of grown-up people. A friend remembered that when she was about twelve, her father had fallen through the roof, badly cutting his leg, and needing skin grafts. One day her seven year old brother said to Mum, 'I'm fed up that Dad's not here, I'm going to pray he'll come home tomorrow.' Without a pause, he went on, 'Dear Jesus, I want my daddy back tomorrow. Thank you. Amen.' There was no suggestion this was possible, so who inspired his prayer? The next day, when Dad did come home, the boy greeted him with a 'Hi Dad!' as if that was obviously the natural outcome.

Children have this implicit trust in a prayer-answering God. Our part is to let the Holy Spirit guide us to guide them as they pray. Together, with the adults in the family, they can learn how the Spirit guides our prayer life, and discover for themselves that he is able to touch people and situations. As we read God's word, so the Spirit interprets it to our needs. Equally, children can have deep experiences of God's Spirit working in them. The difference between them and us, often, is the way they expect this to happen. A five year old girl I know asked her dad, 'Does Jesus live inside me?' 'Yes,' he replied. 'Oh that's a relief,' she went on, 'I thought I was getting fat.'!

'Does Jesus live inside me?'

We need to look positively to the Holy Spirit to lead our prayers, and to claim his power over the evils we face in our difficult lives. We need to believe that, as we pray, so we then go out in the power of the Holy Spirit. As our children grow, we must encourage them to see the Spirit working through them, as he does (or should be doing) through us. And we must not panic if this lesson is a hard one to teach. A delightful three year old friend was sharing the family prayer time. 'Why are you so quiet?' she asked Dad. 'I'm listening to Jesus to hear his answer to my prayer, and waiting for him to speak with me.' Another long pause led to the inevitable question, 'What's he said?' to which he had to reply, 'I don't know!'

What a great anti-climax! Prayer can be fun, and that is part of its being real. But to find out when and where we can do all this praying, let's move on.

5

The where and the when

'All my possessions for a moment of time.' Poor Queen Elizabeth I, saying those words as she died. She would have given *everything* to have had more time! Many of us feel the same when it comes to prayer: if only there was time for it. So much to do, and so little time to stop for family, and God, as we fill our lives up with everything but the most important things. I went to some of the busiest people I know, and asked them where and when they managed to squeeze a space into their lives for praying together as families.

Set times

The regular 'where' and 'when' depends on the style of a particular family. There are those who love a little luxury: 'In the morning, our teenagers come into our bedroom. We all have a cup of tea, read *Living Light* (Kingsway) and they pray with us.' If that was our family, we would have tea everywhere, and our teenagers would lie down and go back to sleep! But if that family can do it, it must be possible.

Then there are the very organised, whose routine is, 'We pray at breakfast, round the table in the kitchen, 7.45am.' There was no suggestion that 7.40 or 7.50 was an alternative! In stark contrast was the answer: 'In any room, *ad hoc.*'

Some families would have tea everywhere . . .

Delving into this somewhat nebulous response, I gleaned that 'any room' meant anywhere downstairs, and *ad hoc* meant usually the second half of the day, often at tea-time, or during the evening, and at times of special appreciation, thanks, concern, or when the needs of others became apparent.

The important thing for each of these families was that the time and place worked well for *them*. That is the key. We each need to find a personal style for our unique family. In talking with dozens of families, mealtimes are by far the most popular times for praying together. Some would say that breakfast is the only possible time, and even that is difficult. Some relatives of ours pray then, but things are complicated by Dad going off to work early sometimes, the eldest doing a paper round, some of the older children lying in, the three year old distracting the others, and a general lack of enthusiasm on occasions. What a set of hindrances, but they persevere. No one said it would be easy.

Another family who pray at breakfast, also share the problem of the youngest not being able to sit still. The mum told

47

me that praying together sometimes works, and sometimes doesn't, but, 'We don't get twitched up on the times when it doesn't work'. They all feel it is important to commit the day to God, even if all they do is grab a few seconds to acknowledge each other to him. I like that, and our family has worked on the breakfast style, using the three or four minutes before the first person leaves (which is also, hopefully, after the last one has made it to the kitchen table).

This bringing each other to God in front of one another is a special moment. Another relative will stand with his family in the hall as he leaves for work, because breakfast is too early for those who will be leaving well after him. Because of this problem, others would opt for the other end of the day. One busy household found mornings to be hopeless, and so pray as a family just before the youngest goes to bed. They shifted their routine from mornings when primary school days ended. Bedtime certainly works for some, especially if the children are not too far apart in age, and thus share a similar end of day routine. This is a particularly good time for very small children, as it gets them into the practice of praying as a fitting conclusion to each day.

Going back to mealtimes, many families find breakfast too rushed, and the day's end too divided, so would use the evening meal as their together time, with each other and with God. An extended grace may be the ideal way to pray, and this can happen at any meal, depending on the chaos, or the opportunity. But don't forget, a semi-cold meal will not be appreciated by anyone, especially the one who has worked hard to get it ready, only to find it dying as an over-enthusiastic prayer goes on and on!

Perhaps those who talk through the meal, and pray afterwards, have a good system. Quite a lot of slightly older families do this, sharing food and conversation, which leads quite naturally into one or more commending the family's life and concerns to God. And if the daily evening meal proves a problem, then the weekend may give a bit more space, and a relaxed Sunday lunch or tea may be the best time to conclude with a reading and a prayer.

Of course, a 'set time' can also happen as and when certain things occur, and so be triggered, not by the time, but by the event. Thus one family I know prays if a phone call brings news which should be brought to God in prayer. Another family sets aside a specific time on certain days, or comes together to pray at times of crisis, or illness. That family sees their set time as being 'whenever it seems appropriate', and they sometimes just stand and pray together wherever they are. I like this spontaneous approach, as long as those who adopt it remember to do it. Not having a routine can lead to praying rarely, or never, but it can also make prayer more real with a 'want to' rather than a 'have to' element. Not being too legalistic is vital.

From time to time sitting down to talk about the best time and place for family prayers is a good idea. Every family's routine changes gradually to suit circumstances and age. But there is one very special time worth a little thought . . .

Birth times

Babies are special! A birth gives a great opportunity to bring God into the very centre of our family life. I even have some friends who shyly, and privately, admit they prayed about their children before they were conceived – at least, about the ones they intended to have, as the last was a bit of a surprise!

There is a beautiful intimacy in praying with an unborn child, and it can be especially important for the dad-to-be, helping him to become more aware of the reality of the new life growing inside his wife's body. Together, the parents can commend their unborn child to God, praying for his Holy Spirit to fill that child from day one. If the greatest thing we long for our children is that they should know the love of Jesus, and have an eternal relationship with the living God, we cannot begin to pray for them too soon.

When it comes to the birth itself, it's a joy and a relief to know God is around! Parents should delight in taking their baby in their arms and dedicating this new life to God, and it is the most normal thing in the world to give thanks for a safe delivery, and the wonder of a brand new human being. I know one dad who even read to his wife, as she was giving birth, some comforting words from the Bible beginning 'Fear not'! Maybe not everyone would find this helpful! Still, one of the most universal reactions to birth is to want to say 'thank you' to someone, and Christians are privileged to know who that someone is.

'Fear not'!!!

If, for any reason, the birth does not go as planned, then there is even more reason to pray as a new family. One close friend told me of her son's premature birth. She and her husband had prayed for him in the womb, and his weight at birth was little more than a bag of sugar. He was in an incubator in a baby unit for nearly four months, during which time his heart stopped beating twice, and he was literally brought back from death. In that dire situation, his parents and a wide circle of family and friends prayed earnestly. They put a notice on the incubator, 'Let everything that has breath praise the Lord', the last verse of Psalm 150. As he came off his breathing apparatus, they prayed he would know God's breath in him. In an emergency operation, they prayed that the Holy Spirit would indeed be for him the 'Paraclete', the one who comes alongside to help. Now a teenager, he still has a strong idea of God being especially close to those who are ill.

As life goes on, whether the baby is well or ill, it is lovely for a family to gather the new child in their arms and pray with him or her. In so doing, we mirror our loving heavenly Father, about whom it is said:

> 'He tends his flock like a shepherd: he gathers the lambs in his arms and carries them close to his heart; he gently leads those that have young' (Isaiah 40:11).

We can pray with our children, and over them, each day, giving them back to God, that they might be his. In so doing, they will learn about prayer in the most wonderful and natural way.

The only regrets I found, as I talked this over with families, were either that they had not done this, or that they had gradually let those early-day prayers slowly fade away. There is no reason why we should stop this praying, and we can ask God to bless our children, whatever their ages. One way is to work out a bedtime routine early on, and then stick with it.

Bedtimes

Some of the people who told me they had let those early prayer times slip away now have children who do not pray at bedtime. They wish their children did pray. Children like a routine. The father of a small girl told me that theirs is very simple: a story – any story, milk, prayer, teeth, good-night! Bringing God into things naturally is the way to do it. A lifetime of personal walking with God cannot begin too soon.

When children are very small, the family's main prayer time may be in their bedroom each evening, especially with under fives. Most families try to fit in a bedtime story, and that can lead naturally into praying. The story books can be supplemented by simple Bible aid books, which are available for all ages. A child is missing a great deal if he or she has never discovered the fun of reading the Bible with *Find out about . . .* , *Quest, One to One* (Scripture Union) and *Topz* (CWR), or of praying with a little help from the brilliant *Lion Book of Children's Prayers*.

Mum and Dad might just learn something too, as they see the splendours of great Bible stories each evening through the eyes of a child, whose mind is uncluttered with the teaching of years. And who should instruct a child in the earliest knowledge of God if not a parent? These are precious times, and should be treasured. Of course each child, and each parent, will differ in the way they like things done. One will want to sing, another to read, a third to lie quietly. A child may want to pray in front of Mum, but not Dad, preferring him to say the prayer. Sometimes the family will share, or a child may want to pray one-to-one with a parent, even if there are other children in the room: it is their personal, special time. Cuddling prayers are allowed, too!

One or two short 'set' prayers, which can be repeated each bedtime, may help a child feel secure. In our home, we have prayed with each of our children a prayer from my own childhood:

> Lord, keep us safe this night,
> Secure from all our fears.
> May angels guard us while we sleep
> Till morning light appears.

One of the major aims of this bedtime praying is for children to develop their own relationship with God which will last beyond the shared praying, as they move from a 'together faith' to a personal, owned faith. Thus an agreed transition will have to come, at a time when the child wishes it. It is almost impossible to set an age at which this happens. One parent told me that he and his wife prayed with their daughters till they were about eight, and then the girls carried on on their own. Others put the change-over age at ten or eleven, whilst at least one family continues this bedtime routine with their fifteen year old daughter, and, on an irregular basis, with their eighteen year old son!

The basic rule is, stop when they want, not when the parents decide. It is quite normal to ask the question, and not to feel hurt if the answer is, 'I'll do it by myself now.' A good time to make this change could be half-way through some Bible notes, so the reading naturally goes on. We have always paid for our children's notes, and been glad when they have moved on to a more senior series. For a while we would ask, 'Have you read your Bible?' but eventually it has to be up to them. There must be a difference between the family praying and the older child praying privately. The former is the way the home does it, whilst the latter is for individual decision: all disciples of Jesus are volunteers. We can pray: we must not pry, or pressurise.

Parents ought not to forget their own bedtime praying, or at least make sure they have their own time with God sometime in the day. We cannot expect our children to do what we say, if we don't do it! A friend of mine gets up early each day to pray, and has been joined recently by his small, lively daughter, who sits with him. What a great lesson she is learning, as she sees Dad at one with his heavenly Father.

Any time

Most Christians would like to get to the point where prayer is the normal, natural thing to do, both individually and as families. Then our praying would be what we *are*, not just what we *do*. It was good to meet many families, when preparing this book, who are beginning to make that a reality.

'Do you pray at other times?' I asked. Very often the answer was, 'Yes,' and the first favourite other time was when they were in the car! There were various reasons for this. One family would entrust their house to the protection of angels as they drove away. Many would pray for safety on the journey, especially if the weather was adverse, or a child was likely to be car sick. Others would use the journey to sing, with praise tapes blaring out. I liked one father's story of a local car journey with his seven year old son. In a hurry to get to the printers, they needed a parking place. They decided to pray, father saying to his son, 'You pray, I'll drive.' The seven year old at once said, 'Please can we have a parking place? Amen.' There was the place, right in front of the printers. 'Thank you.' A week later, Dad heard his son, at home, telling God he'd lost a certain toy, and would he please help him find it. That's how we learn what real prayer is.

The more I asked, the more I realised how much a car is a place of prayer. A friend related how his wife had been taken ill. The doctor said she had to go immediately into hospital. It was Friday evening rush hour and the hospital in question was across London. As they set off, they prayed they would be able to get through the traffic, before it was too late. Park Lane should have been at a standstill, but the whole way cleared and her life was saved. A single friend, who shares his home with several others, told me how one member of his extended family was found by the police, seriously ill in his car. The police phoned my friend and before he and other family members drove off to see if the sick man was even still alive at the hospital, they gathered to pray. Not knowing what to say, the prayer was simply, 'Lord, I pray that somehow he will be aware of your presence.' It later transpired that the first thing the hospital doctor had done was to hold the man's hand and say, 'God loves you.'

Sometimes the car itself causes the crisis which brings

about a cry to God for help. An evangelist colleague was travelling in Poland with his son when, unknown to them, their document case fell out as a door was opened. Two hundred miles further on, they realised their loss. My colleague read these words:

> We know that in all things God works for the good of those who love him (Romans 8:28).

Then father and son prayed together for help. Four days later they returned to the huge city where they thought they might have lost the case. The first policeman they spoke to was a mate of a policeman who had found the documents, and he took them to meet him.

One more car story, where the car was also the problem, and where God was the answer. A man from our church had his car stolen from outside his own house. His four year old daughter said, 'We must pray for the car to be found by Father God.' Half a mile away, in a pub car park, there was the car, undamaged. Even the police could hardly believe it. When the man took his daughter to see it she was very pleased, but not at all surprised.

Whatever the crisis, it can encourage 'any time' praying. One of my relatives always prays with her children when they see an ambulance, that God will help whoever is being rushed to hospital. One family prays when the news on television is particularly bad. Another prays in the car each time they have been to see their sick gran in hospital. Illness will often encourage an immediate prayer, as will an emergency, whether the crisis belongs to the family or to someone known to them. A nightmare will need a prayer, and so will an exam, or a spelling test! 'We prayed at the funfair when the children were terrified,' said one mum. 'We pray before our daughter goes horse-riding,' said another.

'Any time' praying can embrace the best in life, too. Setting off on holiday, or going for a walk, are times for prayer. Glorying in God's creation should lift the heart of young and old, even if it is only a 'Wow, isn't God brilliant!' When a good thing happens, we should want to thank God there and then. When a small boy I know was given a one pound coin, he managed to lose it right out of his hand straight away. He prayed with his parents as to its where-abouts. In a cafe, just as he wanted to spend it, it fell out of his sleeve. 'Thanks, Lord!'

My favourite 'any time' story came from a family which is rapidly growing up and leaving home. Whenever one of them goes off to university, the whole family stands on the railway station platform sharing a big hug, and they pray out loud for the one who is going. They don't care who watches!

The best time

Throughout this chapter there have been dozens of examples of times and places when and where people pray. Each one of us needs to go for the ones which are for us, and not to panic that others do things differently. It is worth realising that even those who seem to have got things 'perfect' change their routines, and circumstances will mean that we need to adjust. When I asked one friend if his family rang the changes he replied, 'All the time!'

Changes may be deliberate, or just happen, almost by accident. If a serious routine is needed, hang on to it. If the family feels good with its style, that's a good indication that you've got it right. And, if you're only at the stage of getting started, let's think about how to do just that.

PART TWO

Go for it!

6

Getting started

'We'd love to pray together as a family. But how do we start?'
Let's pick up a few tips from those who are actually doing it.

Early starts

'We'd prayed together before we started going out,' one lady
told me. You can't start earlier than that! She and her hus-
band-to-be carried on praying together whilst they were
going out, and then on into their marriage, and during
pregnancy. 'It was natural to pray as a family, we just went
on doing what we always had done.' This couple aren't out-
of-touch, 'super-spiritual' types, but a terrific, outgoing pair,
with a great home and vibrant lives. They know that, with
God, they can build the best possible life, and they are not
ashamed to go for that.

Other couples start praying together well before they get
married, so that daily prayers continue to be the norm for
their family life when children arrive. And if the 'going out'
phase has not been the time to start, others begin a lifetime
of praying as a family on the honeymoon. Many a couple
would say they are glad that they had made a habit of praying
together before their first child was born.

Often it is only the initial fear of embarrassment which
stops people praying together. The first efforts are the hardest,

and feel the worst. We dread looking stupid, and that is where the trust of a loving relationship helps. We need to be honest about, for example, our shyness of praying out loud, and then to ask for the other's help. Praying as a loving, caring couple is a great way to begin a family prayer time. This is so whether the two are not yet married, or have been for many years. Surely we can be less fearful with our most loved person than with anyone else? Then when we want to bring in the children, or other family members and friends, that partner will be there to back us up.

And if we need an excuse, a new baby gives the perfect reason for praying as a family. 'Father, thank you for this wonderful gift,' may be the start of an ongoing prayer life. One dad proudly told me how he and his wife had prayed 'from day one when our first child was born.' He went on to tell me how this seemed so natural, and evolved into prayers at bedtimes and mealtimes. Once a start is made, it is actually difficult not to go on. The best way to avoid embarrassment with what the children will think is to start before they realise what is happening! If they are prayed with when they are tiny, they will grow up accepting that this is a normal part of the family's life. Why wait till there are three or four children before making a start? A couple is a family. Parent and child is a family. Whoever lives under the one roof can be a family. The eldest will miss out if we wait, so we can and should pray with him or her at once.

If birth seems too early, some parents begin family praying as soon as they feel their first child is able to understand something of what is going on. A child does seem to have an instinctive awareness of God and, though it may be harder for us, praying will be quite natural to little ones. One mum told me that her small children expected prayer to happen, as part of the daily routine. Bedtime was not complete without a prayer, and it was not quite right to eat a meal without giving thanks. By building in this expectation, a child will make prayer happen, even when we don't want to pray, or can't bring ourselves to.

Especially at times of illness, what is more comforting than to hold a little child in a caring embrace, and pray for God's help? That was the trigger for one family to start their praying together, and things went on from there. Though the mum also related how her two year old would get up three times during an evening so they could pray about her headache! There was some doubt about whether this was, in fact, just a splendid way to extend the time before finally settling down to sleep!

. . . her two year old would get up three times during an evening so they could pray about her headache!

'Why don't we?'

One dad I met told me how when he visited other peoples' homes, he had seen families praying together. He thought about it and then asked his wife why on earth they didn't pray in their home. So, one evening, he simply sat down with the family and said a prayer. It was as straightforward as that. The children didn't say 'No!', he was relieved to find, though the only prayers they had ever heard up till then had been at their Sunday groups. No one had prayed in front of them apart from that, and certainly not their parents. The mum added that she was glad when Dad did this, as she had just been thinking of the story of Hannah and her son Samuel, and of how God had been in their relationship.

When an already existing family want to start praying together, the best way to get going is just to do it. If the children are old enough to understand, talking it through will help to make it a joint decision which everyone owns. If a parent expresses a need for prayer, the children are more likely to agree with the idea. 'I'm under a lot of pressure at the moment, gang. I want your help – would you pray with me for God to strengthen me?' Who could resist that (as long as it is true!)?

Afterwards, others in the family will probably be more willing to say when they need similar help, and so prayer becomes a form of mutual support, as well as bringing in the great added dimension of God. An honest discussion is a starter. Families need to talk with each other. Similarly, when a new older person joins an existing family set-up, talking about the changes it means will help. A single friend of mine had a family move in with him (he had a big house, and they had nowhere). He was used to praying anyway, and they were also a family which prayed together. But when this new extended family came into being, they needed to agree together that it would be good to meet as a new unit to pray.

God has a hand in all this, too! We often assume we are making the move, when all the time he is prompting our minds. A keen Christian I know realised he was just too busy for his family. He would see his children asleep in bed and pray for them then. He began to wish he could pray with them, too, as his wife did when she put them to bed. He told me how his conscience was troubled about this. And so each week the family decided to carve out a time when they could all be together and, as part of their special 'sharing time', pray with and for each other. If we are determined enough, we will probably be able to find the time and space for whatever we really want somewhere.

Perhaps it comes as we are more aware of God, and as he works in a deeper way in our lives. One couple told me how, after eight or nine years of marriage, God became more real to them, and they were aware of their need to pray, and so began to set aside time to pray together. 'It meant disciplining ourselves to do something,' they admitted. Even keen Christians would say that praying is not easy – but it is vital, and wonderful.

'Now we're Christians . . .'

For some families, it is when Mum or Dad become Christians that prayer becomes real for them and their children. Families will often have times together whatever their spiritual state, and whether they involve God or leave him out altogether. For one family I know, the evening story-time and sharing time was important well before God got a look in. When they started to go to church, and ultimately became Christians, they began to tell their children stories from the Bible. Out of the good things that brought, a prayer time naturally developed. Then prayer became more about their own personal lives, as they talked with God. 'We knew nothing to begin with,' they told me. But what a great way to learn, as together they allowed God's love to enhance all they already did. When prayer flows naturally, it is at its very best.

The opposite is also true: forced prayer can be a terrible pain, and put people off. Shortly after a colleague of mine became a Christian, some if his friends expressed surprise that he did not pray with his family. Their insensitivity created an adverse pressure, which he found very unhelpful. Instead of helping the family, it actually stopped them praying together for some time. Their judgmental approach got in the way, and he now sees the danger of his over-reaction.

Happily, God did lead him gently on, and with the Holy Spirit's help the family finally got around to their prayers. We mustn't let others put us off!

Often, there may be many steps along the way to a whole family praying together, especially if some become Christians before others. I talked with one family where once upon a time there was no prayer in the home at all, not even with the children when they were small. When Mum became a Christian, she started to pray with each child individually as she put them to bed. When her husband also became a Christian two years later, they were then all able to pray together each evening, as Mum and Dad shared in the routine of putting their children to bed. Alas, the local church then saw Dad as a great asset, and got him involved in so many things that the family prayer time was jeopardised! They had to work very hard to keep afloat this very special new feature of their life together. In our church life we need to be careful to allow families their own time.

Overcoming hang-ups

Some people have a very real barrier in their lives which can prove almost impassable when it comes to making family prayers happen. For example, some people's background or upbringing makes them feel that praying out loud should never be done, or should only be done by a minister, or men, or adults. How can someone like this break free from the restrictions they feel weigh heavily upon them? It may take some courage, and a great deal of support and understanding from others within the household. A desire to pray, and a belief that it is right, are vital. But it may well be very hard at first.

Perhaps as we look at a not dissimilar hang-up, the answer to this first one may emerge. Earlier I mentioned a friend of mine with an over-aggressive father, whose prayers were both formal and unloving. When this man felt he would like to lead his own family in prayer, all he could think of were his father's domineering practices. What he did in the end was to call a family conference. He explained that he longed for them to pray together, and then told them the whole story of his own childhood, and how the horror of long, boring, meaningless daily prayers haunted his mind. His children were shocked: 'Don't do that here!' they said.

'I don't want to introduce a stiff, inflexible system,' he replied, 'but I do want us to relate to God, and pray together.' Would they help him with his phobia, please? They *did* understand, and a very *ad hoc* style of praying together took off from that day. The family made sure that prayer did happen, in a style which suited all of them, especially Dad. Best of all, the children didn't make a big deal of it, and took this new aspect of family life in their stride. Several years later, Dad is happy to say that his family prayers are 'relevant, but not heavy'.

I am sure that this style of dealing with our difficulties is the best way to get them out of the way. When the Bible talks about 'carry[ing] each other's burdens' (Galatians 6:2), it surely includes this sort of situation too. Whatever the problem regarding praying, a loving family and God can work it through, and work it out.

Some practicalities

One of the best pieces of advice I have ever heard on this whole subject was, 'Start as you mean to go on'. One of the families mentioned earlier made that a deliberate policy from day one. They decided that a couple of minutes at breakfast each day stood a better chance than anything else – at least for them – hence the famous 'Breakfast, in the kitchen, 7.45am'. As they have done this most successfully for twenty or more years, who can say they were anything but spot on?

It is therefore worth thinking through the 'How often?' question as a first priority, especially if the family is rarely together. Coupled with this, is the 'How long?' problem, which will partly be governed by the youthfulness of the children. If there is no wild enthusiasm, a weekly three minutes to kick off may be more realistic than half-an-hour at tea-time each day! The family can then talk about the 'What shall we do?' question. As each person shares their ideas, a unique pattern for the family will emerge, and each will feel they have contributed to the scheme, and own what happens.

By so doing, each of the first few prayer times will be an adventure, a discovery of being together in a brand new way, and of bringing God to the very heart of family life. Of course, a great deal of care will be needed to see that each family member fits in. An older family will be very different from one with toddlers. The latter may want energetic action choruses, whilst the former will (with teenagers leading) want to collapse in the most comfortable chairs and let Dad, or Mum, do it all!

We find that, even on those days when we don't have a prayer time, we are at least able to share a 'thank you' prayer before each meal. As the later section on graces will show, this need not be a burden before getting down to eating, and can encourage a God-awareness in a very simple way.

Whatever our circumstances, there is no time like the present, and no place like home, to begin this adventure of praying together. Let's not leave God out any longer!

Ah, but you don't know *my* situation . . . Then we'd better look at it right away.

Toddlers may want energetic action choruses . . . teenagers may want to collapse in the most comfortable chairs and let Dad and Mum do it all.

7

But what if . . .?

The theory of praying together is great. Unfortunately situations and people in real life can make the turning of that theory into practice a serious problem. This chapter and the next two aim to help us face the difficulties, and find some answers.

When facing any tricky moment, I am always reminded of something I heard Corrie ten Boom say: 'God has no problems, only plans. There is no panic in heaven.' Whatever we may see as a hindrance, God knows the way through or round.

'I don't want to pray!'

In some families, no one has ever said this, even as the children have grown older. Perhaps they are exceptional! But it is certainly worth working hard to find a system with which everyone does feel comfortable. A relaxed approach lets anyone who, for whatever reason, does not want to pray on a particular day, say so. Hopefully, that person will then feel comfortable staying with the family, even if they don't pray. This style may avoid a crisis, and enable the praying to go on anyway. In our home, if on a rare occasion, someone says 'No' when asked to pray, we move at once to another and ask them instead. As time goes by we have learned to discern if one of our children does not feel like praying aloud, and quietly leave them alone.

As a friend told me, 'If they don't want to pray, they don't. We pray for them, and thank God for what he is doing for them. If people are not speaking to each other or to God it doesn't prevent their being prayed for.' Taking the sting out of a possible crisis must be the immediate way. Even if this were to go on over a period of time, what is the point of forcing someone to pray out loud? Everyone has to find their own way and God has more subtle methods of warming hearts than we do. They may sit with their eyes open waiting for prayer time to finish, but at least they are being included in the family circle. Some families plan their prayer times so they are fairly difficult to avoid. If prayers are immediately before breakfast, people are likely to be there.

Sooner or later, if an older child consistently refuses to participate, a caring parent will want to know if something is wrong. The question then is, what would that parent do with *any* difficulty being faced by a family member? If the usual family way of dealing with problems is a head–on confrontation, perhaps now is the time to alter that style! Most parents would find a good time in private to ask if all was not well, and whether they could do anything to help. I know some parents who have done that when prayer is the issue. I like this approach. It gives the parent the chance to share honestly how he or she has found praying to be a problem, if this is the case.

Some families I have met ask reluctant participants to leave the room. How do they react? Here's what one mum said: 'The little one throws himself on the floor, the ten year old storms out and slams the door, while the big ones look resigned and hold hands!' I think I'd be looking for a slightly less exclusive system!

In chapter three I mentioned briefly another style of deal-ing with this problem. The young daughter in this family made it very plain she did not want to join in. She would sit and pretend to do other things, as her parents tried to help her understand that God loved her and wanted her to talk to him. In the end, she would hide the daily reading book, hoping that would ruin the prayer time. Her parents rose to the challenge, inventing a special game of hide-and-seek to find the book. Everyone joined in, much to the daughter's delight. Of course, when the book was found, she discovered she was now part of family prayers! Prayer time from then on incorporated hide-and-seek. The other ploy they used was to tell the little girl, 'Don't listen to this, do something else.' The reading would become irresistible.

A more difficult problem arises when it is a parent who does not want to pray. 'If I don't want to pray,' one dad told me, 'I just don't. My wife prays on her own!' This may work occasionally, but family prayers are in danger of slowly failing if such an approach continues. One parent told me, 'There were times when I didn't pray, because I couldn't get myself together for breakfast, which was our best time. The children pushed for us to pray, but it began to slip away. Family prayers never really took off because my wife and I didn't make them.' A cautionary tale, and one I know rings bells with me.

Some families do stop praying together because people simply don't want to, but often the main reason is because the adults in the family don't take a lead in making prayer happen. Another dad told me how easy it was to busy himself with other things if he did not want to be involved. If it is the children who, at their secondary school stage, rebel, then prayers can continue for them, even if they physically absent themselves from the prayer time. One mum said she always assured her daughters she would pray for them every day as they went out, and that each knew this did happen. In another similar situation, the oldest daughter would sit obviously objecting to being involved in the prayer time, and it was agreed with this sixteen year old that it was not helpful for her or for the rest of the family to insist she be present for prayers. She was allowed to opt out, yet knew she would be prayed for.

Occasionally, the difficult decision may have to be made to stop praying together as a family because none of the children wants to continue. I only met one family where this had happened. Dad is an ordained minister, so the whole family's life revolved round God and the church. The pressure to be 'spiritual' was always there. When the children were small, it was easy to pray together but, as they got older, resentment set in. A conscious decision was made that it was not worth flogging a dead horse. The parents found their decision a hard one to make, partly feeling they should continue. The parents still prayed with the children individually for a while, until they got older. After that, the children even resented being asked if they had prayed privately: 'It's up to me. What's it got to do with you?' The parents realised that the children were feeling claustrophobic: they lived in the minister's house; they were known as 'the minister's kids' at school; and they needed space. By laying off, the parents are now discovering that when they talk to their children about a particular crisis and say, 'We've been praying about that,' the children will respond, 'So have we.'

Each family will have to work out this tricky problem of some people not wanting to pray, and part of the answer may be how we cope with people feeling embarrassed, or getting bored . . .

'It's embarrassing . . . and boring!'

Usually it is embarrassment *or* boredom, so let's look at embarrassment first. People do sometimes feel embarrassed when they pray out loud. The best thing seems to be to pass on quickly and not make a big thing of it, so that embarrassment does not turn to hardness, or even to hatred of prayer. In our home, we would never let anyone mock another's prayer. And, though we might smile at an interesting turn of phrase, we would make sure it was clear we were in sympathy with the person who said it, not that we were getting at them.

When people have anxieties they may feel embarrassed about sharing them. Some parents pray with a child individually in such situations. Honesty is a great help, and it is lovely if a child, or a parent, can say, 'I didn't find that prayer easy.' It may help to remind an embarrassed family member that their prayers *do* matter, and are important. Equally, it is wise not to intrude into someone's problems till that person feels comfortable about sharing them with others. The embarrassment may not be with a child but with an adult, especially when emotional matters arise, or we feel inadequate, and our family discovers the real person behind the mask. We must beware of double standards, forcing a child to be totally open in prayer, however embarrassing that may be, whilst hiding ourselves away when the prayer is too tricky for us.

How we react in potentially embarrassing situations will speak silent volumes to our children. This is never more apparent than when we have others from outside our nuclear family present. In chapter three we looked at some of the joys and problems of visitors being present at family prayer times. They can also be a source of embarrassment. Should the family say grace when visitors are present? Children need a better reason for not saying grace than the fact that Dad would go red! One family I talked with was sensible enough to acknowledge to each other that they did get embarrassed when visitors were there at their prayer time. They then agreed that it was important to carry on, as their prayers were with God, and not to impress others. However, they kept the prayers shorter and not too intimate, so that neither they nor the visitors felt embarrassed.

If embarrassment is solved by discretion and tact, boredom is solved by brevity and variety. 'Keep it short and sweet,' families tell me. 'Keep it fresh,' others say, or, 'Our prayers aren't long enough for us to get bored!' Others agree that their prayers can occasionally be boring, and when they dry up someone will say, 'Let's have breakfast!' which saves the day.

Most families make sure there is no time to be bored.

They keep the prayer time informal, and always have a reason for praying. I was told by one family, 'We don't come to "wait on the Lord", or to wait for a prophetic utterance, we come to talk about something, not to meditate.' They were not saying there was *never* a time for these things, but that they were not appropriate for their family prayer time, as they may have caused boredom.

The easy-going approach seems to be the answer to boredom. Ringing the changes helps some families, and being sensitive to each other's needs is important too. Our family finds that making prayer relevant is the secret, to deal with the immediacy of each day. Some families play games, and ask questions about the reading. Honest praying, and a fresh and personal phraseology, keep the prayers from getting stereotyped and predictable. It is occasionally worth reminding the family what an honour it is to pray, and to be part of a Christian family, even if prayer does seem 'the same as usual'. Thinking of the wonderful God we are praying to, and of how he longs to hear from us, can help any boredom be lifted.

We find it hardest to avoid prayer being boring when we are tired, and the burden of responsibility to make praying interesting rests on a weary parent. It is tempting to stop for a while, and to re-start when it will be less boring: but who knows when that will be? Persevering may be hard, but it's worth it.

8

Different people

Prayer means people! With some people, we may have to work out special ways to help our prayers happen. For a start, what are we to do if one or more members of our family is not yet a Christian?

'They're not Christians'

In some families, where only one person would claim to be a Christian, family prayers would seem very unlikely. 'We don't pray as a family, because they are not committed,' one lady told me. 'There's only me – and my sister living nearby. The family know that we pray. I told my daughter I was praying for her. She was pleased, but she'd be embarrassed if we prayed together. The family accepts that I'm a Christian.' Sometimes, we need to be patient, keep quiet, and let God work in our families.

Another lady told me how her non-Christian son had been glad to pray with her at the breakfast table as he came up to his exams, as he was at a special time of need. But if, for example, a teenage daughter deliberately turns her back on God, it will only make things worse if a parent tries to continue involving her in the family's prayer times. Parents have to be sensible enough to recognise when teenagers need to make their own way. However, a simple grace at meal times is worth hanging on to.

If the majority of a family wants to pray and, say, one teenage son wishes to opt out, the rest of the family may well still find times to pray together. If prayer is at breakfast time, that son may choose to come to the meal late. The alternative is to carry on, with prayer being as much the norm as the meal itself. But any decision must be made with loving concern for all family members, and especially for those who are away from God.

The problem may become insurmountable if one of the adults in the family is not yet a Christian, and here very great sensitivity and tact will be needed. A Christian partner will long for their husband or wife to know and love Christ too. One lady told me, 'I never talk to my husband about Christian things. I know I'm not the right person, so the best thing is not to. If *I* tried to talk to him, I'd put him off.' Because of this approach, her husband is willing to come to church with her on special occasions: 'He comes to church as I would go to a football match, not to enjoy it but to be "family" together.' I like that! One of her sons is a keen Christian, and the two of them agree to pray about things in their individual, private prayers, but they also agree that to be seen praying together would be difficult. 'I used to worry about all this,' she says, 'but I prayed about it, and I see now that this is the best way for us at present.'

There are some who would want to try to pray with the family despite a non-Christian partner, but it can be awkward. If the Christian partner prays with the children at bedtime, then the other may find it uncomfortable if, when she puts those children to bed, they ask her to pray with them and she feels she can't. The more gentle the approach, the more the partner will warm to Christian things. However, small children in particular find bedtime prayers so enjoyable and helpful that these should not lightly be abandoned. I know at least one dad who always prays with the children at bedtime, and at other times when his wife is not there. 'She's a bit mocking!' he told me, 'But I don't push it. We pray if things go wrong, or if we have things to thank God for. My wife knows we do, but she never mentions it. I keep praying for her.'

Some non-Christian partners make no objection to a family prayer time. Even if that partner has no faith, he or she may feel that there is value in the children having involvement with God and the church. One lady told me, 'My husband encourages the children to go to church and to pray. He's happy for me to pray with the children, and supports my Christian life.' This particular man wants to be sincere, but will not pretend he is what he is not – yet. When his wife was ill, he was prepared to go with the children to church, despite the fact that he felt uncomfortable. As long as his wife does not presume on his support, he is happy that she keeps the Christian side of the family going.

In some homes, even more may be possible. If the partners have a good, loving relationship, healthy conversation about spiritual things can take place, and partners will want to support each other in every way. In those circumstances, I know of families where they do have family prayers, and they go to church together, even when one partner is not a Christian. In such a family the Christian partner will be able to pray with the children each night, and the other partner may be prepared to do so as well. Grace may be welcome, and the innocent questioning by the children may be an effective way of getting through to the adult who isn't a Christian.

It does seem that quite a lot is possible. I have been both surprised and pleased to find so many families where a very positive style is working. Gentleness, love, openness and honesty seem to be the most vital ingredients. Even though the non-Christian partner could be viewed as a 'problem', sometimes it is not a help to see it this way. After all, we all have things which others would like to change in us. The thing is never to despair, and to trust God for his timing to change the situation: our partner is not a problem for him.

We need to remember, God loves that person much more than we do, and trust him accordingly.

'What about the "extended" family?'

'We had a friend stay with us – he was very private. He wouldn't come to our family prayers, but he would join in prayer at meals. We let him decide what to do.' That's how one family described to me what happened in their home. And that 'no pressure' style seems to be the one most adopt if their family is joined for any length of time by an 'outsider'.

Lodgers need to be allowed to live their own lives, and a lodger may well opt out of the breakfast-time prayers of the family with whom they stay. At most, prayer with such a person might cover specific needs only. If he or she is not a Christian, the family might prefer to pray alone. Equally, a Christian might like to take part in a very positive way: so much depends on the extra person in the home. Even with a Christian, it may not feel right for them to join in on a day-to-day basis, partly because their timetable might not fit in with the family, and partly because the intimacy of family praying would be spoilt if the 'extra' was always there.

All the family needs to be in agreement here. The attitude of the children can be crucial. One person may be immediately embraced as 'family', while another could stay for ever and never get in close. Some friends of ours had such a situation with two people who lodged with them for lengthy periods, one after the other. The first young lady seemed to fit in perfectly, and joined in the evening meal prayer times. When the next lady arrived, the young daughter of the family was keen for her *not* to join in family things, and it seemed right to respect her wishes.

In some circumstances it might be extremely desirable not to encourage an extended family member to be around when we pray! When one little girl announced, 'Mummy's been horrible, and she needs to say sorry to God in our prayer time!', Mummy understandably felt glad their guest was not around for that particular moment! It will always depend on both the occasion and the person, and on the sort of prayers to be prayed. That will be so even if the extra person is a close relative, such as a parent of the parents, as even they may inhibit really free prayers.

One person who will often have an extended family is a single man or woman, so . . .

'What if I'm single?'

Where two or three singles share a home, they may want to mould into a 'family' that prays and shares together. They may well find that their prayer times are much better than those of families who are related, and that they have fewer problems with visitors. I would certainly want to encourage Christians sharing a house to pray together if they can. The struggles and good things brought by a family prayer time in this situation are likely to be similar to those in any other family structure.

A single may well take in lodgers, both for reasons of finance and for company. One friend who does this says that she and her lodger will pray about particular issues as the need arises, but not on a regular basis. She prays more regularly with someone else, in her house or theirs, and she also shares in prayer with a couple she knows. With each of these people – her lodger and her friends – she is glad that any of them can take the lead in making the praying happen.

For single people, probably more than for the members of a nuclear family, there needs to be a deliberate commitment to pray in the home. A family prayer time may evolve, whilst single people will need to take positive steps to make a prayer time happen. A single man whom I know well says that each person in the house needs to agree that they are establishing a system of praying as a family together. It is then possible to act and live as a family, though the leading participants are single. He says that this security of commitment gets rid of the uncertainty of, 'Where do I stand?'

Prayer is in some ways easier, because the pressures of the nuclear family are not there.

Far from bemoaning the single state, many value it as giving greater freedom, and that liberty includes the opportunity of praying together with the family at home.

'I'm a single parent'

An increasing number of people are single parents these days. A parish priest told me recently that ninety per cent of the families in his care were one-parent families. A person may not have married, have separated from their partner, have gone through a divorce or a bereavement. We will look at these two latter experiences in the next chapter, but here are a few thoughts on the single aspect.

The majority of single parents caring for children are mums, but many dads have to cope on their own in bringing up a family too. For Mum, or Dad, on their own, there are inevitably special challenges. One parent has to do the work of two, carrying all the responsibilities of the home and family alone. Often this will include doing a full-time job, and means huge pressures on time and energy. This pressure is made worse by the lack of extended families today, compared with even a few years ago. The nuclear family may well be a long way from other relatives, who could have helped had they been just around the corner. For most people, gone are the days when aunts and grannies could be called on to share in the raising of children. A single parent may feel very alone.

Praying may prove one of the great positives here. When Mum or Dad want to pray with the children, there is no one to contradict this decision – there is no difficult partner to disagree! If the single parent wants to start family prayers with small children, they only have to get on and do it. If there are older children, here is the perfect excuse for starting: we need all the help we can get, so let's bring God in on our lives. God is not being used as a substitute partner, but as the one who can help the home to succeed.

This is the experience of many single parents I know. They regard their situation as a special opportunity to show how they rely on God, and so encourage their children to do the same. Whilst there is a danger of using prayer as a weapon against a former partner, the single parents I spoke to told me that, instead, prayer is a great way of emphasising God's goodness, and praising him for his help. Single parents who do pray with their families are surprised how little other people seem to understand the strength of their situation, and see only the apparent problems. Prayer, in the single parent family, works pretty much the same as in other families.

This positive approach is one I also encountered when asking about the last of these 'people' situations . . .

'What about those who are handicapped?'

What happens if someone in the family is handicapped in some way, suffering from a physical or, especially, a mental disability? The major thing is not to see this as a problem, if at all possible. Some families see the disability as a positive bonus. One boy I know who is rather lame is seen both by himself and by his family as proof of God's goodness. This boy all-but died at birth, and his limp is a daily reminder of God's help. 'For us, it is a trophy, not a problem,' says his mum. The way God now blesses the boy, and the family, is compensation for the difficulties.

Even in a family where one partner is not a Christian, a child's handicap will encourage that partner to believe in the Christian partner's prayers, as one family told me. Any lack of ability can stimulate prayer: one husband told me that, as his wife gets progressively more ill, she relies on his prayers, and these have become a vital part of their relationship.

This is not to deny that a handicap can sometimes be a real problem when it comes to praying together as a family. A mentally handicapped child may bring great difficulties when it comes to pitching the prayers for the rest of the family. The able children will grow tired, as they get older, of prayers remaining at too simple a level, whilst the handicapped child may not be able to sit through a Bible reading and extended prayer time. The family may have to split the family praying, with a very simple style for 'all together' times, and something deeper for the more able ones. If the handicapped person is unable to stay quiet during a prayer time, it may be better to pray individually with that child, and with the others.

There will be pressure on time, too. A person who has a physical or mental handicap may need longer to get dressed and to eat meals than other family members, leaving little time for mealtime family prayers. Frequent hospital visits may disrupt the regular routine, and praying may fall by the wayside because it is difficult to arrange. But there may be a greater awareness of human need. And the struggle to find a time to pray may make that time more precious. Often a handicapped person will bring out the very best in family and friends, and that person will show the greatness of God's love, rather than cause the opposite reaction. Crises are bound to arise, and it is often during such times we turn to God most. A handicapped family member can draw us nearer to each other and to God, in prayer.

Whatever the special needs in our families, every one of us has much to give and much to learn. So let's pray about our problems and thank God for each other.

9

Times of pain

Life brings its burdens and griefs to each of us, and we may find there is no time like a time of suffering for crying out to God in prayer. But what if the pain of the situation makes it seem almost impossible for a family to pray together? Let's face some of these hurts, and find a way through.

'Our marriage is over'

Marriage as an institution is in a mess. Many a home will struggle with the basic concept of what a 'father' is, which immediately complicates the first two words of the Lord's Prayer. Marriages of Christians are not exempt from break-down, and that is so even when both partners would say they were committed to the idea of Christian marriage. How can a family's prayers survive the shock of separation and divorce?

Let's not pretend that prayer, in such circumstances, will be anything other than difficult. One mum I spoke with discovered her husband was having an affair while she was pregnant, and her son has never known his father. When the family, without Dad, prays together, they have to think of God in a wholly different way from the usual concept of 'Father'. Mum says she has to turn a deaf ear to her son's prayers sometimes, and hope he will not raise the topic of his dad in prayer. However, Mum's positive attitude has helped her son to find, in God, someone who does care for him, and she shows that the family can keep on praying even though Dad has left.

When a separation first happens it is especially hard to pray, particularly as a family. The hurts are so intense, and life is undergoing such huge changes. Family members struggle merely to survive. If regular praying together ends abruptly, some period of time may have to elapse before this special relationship can resume. Dad or Mum's weekly visit may not help either, and they too may miss the prayers of the family and the spiritual side of home life. The parent who has left, for whatever reason, will have deep hurts. One dad, who had to leave his wife after he had confessed to an affair, told me sadly how he was hoping he would be able to pray again with his son, and how he was finding the loss of family prayers devastating.

As time goes on, the remaining members of the family need to re-establish their togetherness. Here is an opportunity for honesty in prayer, and for each family member to play their part in filling the gap. Forgiveness may take a long time. I was very moved by one family's story. Dad and Mum had divorced, and some while later there was a family baptism, with communion as part of the service. Individual families were invited to receive communion together, and Dad and Mum were brave enough to join with their children for this. The mum told me how the children had seen this as a great step forward, giving them assurance and security. 'I must admit it was some years after the divorce,' she said. Some families might never feel able to get to a similar point, but it was a huge achievement for them.

However desperate the situation, this is a vital time for prayer, and for those who are left in the home to keep praying together if possible. People have shared with me how they drew enormous strength from each other's prayers, and from the God who answered those cries from the heart. 'I felt as if I were being carried along,' one told me, 'and in my new singleness I found the strength I needed.' Now is also the time to lean on others, as they pray with us and for us. In an extended family I know, a non-family resident was able to give the added support in prayer of someone not so immediately caught up in the situation. Another friend was a lodger in a family where Dad had just left, and was able to pray with each person in that home in a way they could not do together because of their hurts.

If eventually, a new partner comes on the scene, a further delicate situation arises, with he or she needing to fit into the family, and its prayer times. It can be, and probably will be, embarrassing at first. The more intimate prayers will take a back seat for a while. For example, the children will find it difficult to talk about their dad or pray for him in the presence of the new partner. In some ways it will have been easier for the one parent plus the children. And it will take a while for the newcomer to feel accepted and included.

Great courage in prayer is needed when a family breaks up. And when a family falls out, quite a bit of courage is needed then as well . . .

'We've had a row!'

Not many families get through their lives without an occasional blow-up, and we all have to learn to cope with differences, problems, arguments and rifts from time to time. For some families, a good old row will stop their joint prayers until it blows over. If the rule is that the family only prays when all can make it, then they will not be able to if someone has gone off in a huff. A bust-up equals no praying. Then, as the dust settles, some will realise that there should have been prayer.

I love those homes where I am told, 'If there's a row, Dad prays and Mum watches'! Or again, 'Someone else will have to do something about it.' Several families I know have adopted as a sort of 'rule of the house' Paul's advice in Ephesians:

> Do not let the sun go down while you are still angry (Ephesians 4:26).

One such family will even wait up for the last one to come home at night to put things right – I hope the little ones can stay awake! And I hope this doesn't become a way to manipulate each other.

This is the sort of time, strangely, that family prayers are made for. Parents speak of the healing brought about by praying after difficulties in the home, and of being able to talk things through, knowing that God is part of this sharing. The prayer may be stilted, but it is sad if those prayers cannot happen at all. At least the family can agree to differ, even if that includes an opt-out from prayers by one family member. And, if just one person has the problem, it may be better sorted out separately, before the family prays.

'Someone has died'

A major loss of someone, or something, is a devastating blow, and can be like a dagger entering the very heart of a family. What happens to prayer at such a time? As creation withdraws at winter to survive, so there is individual and collective withdrawal at a bereavement. Praying together may fizzle out for a while, till the initial shock has passed. Some feel abandoned by God, and need others to pray for them, and on their behalf, as they cannot. In a non-demonstrative family, visible grief at prayer time would be impossible to cope with, and all that is needed is the understanding that each is praying for the other privately. We can comfort each other by this, and accept our inability to join in prayer for a time.

Of course, it is good if we can pray together. We may have been able to pray through a situation before it occurs, for example, praying with and for someone who is dying. As soon as the bereavement happens, many families will pray at once, and the fresh, raw hurts will dominate family prayers. Such a situation will bring an added dimension to those prayer times, and the day of a funeral may bring the most poignant prayers ever expressed together. In the depths of grief this can produce great good for the family, bringing them closer to each other as well as to God.

As time goes by, prayers will be a way of working through grief, enabling us to express our gratitude for the person who has gone, and also come to terms with the experience of bereavement. For a child facing this for the first time, family prayers can be invaluable. We need to be keenly aware of a child's bereavement feelings. Children may need more prayers when their rabbit dies than when an elderly relative does! One family I know well had a dreadful bereavement when three close relatives died together, and the children bombarded their parents with questions. Each question was not only answered, but turned into a prayer. 'Any hurt has to be turned into a prayer,' the grieving mum told me.

This must be the ideal way to handle pain, whatever the loss. Bereavement is not only caused by death, but by any sort of loss. When a family moves to another town, for example, they can talk and pray honestly together about their feelings, and trust God for his help in their loss of friends, and in their loneliness of not knowing anyone. When a parent loses a job, or someone leaves home, or illness debilitates, or any loss comes, the family can unitedly cry to God in their trouble and hurt, and know his binding up and healing. Now is the time, maybe like no other, for bringing God into our family situation.

'The memory hurts'

As the years go by, grief can still continue, and a painful anniversary may need careful handling. For some families, it may be best to leave painful memories alone when praying together. For others, the first Christmas, birthdays and the anniversary of a bereavement may be too traumatic a time to pray together as a family, but there can be the strength of knowing that we are praying for each other privately. A big hug can be prayer enough in itself.

Even after many years, a particular day in the year will be hard for one or more in the family because of some painful event which happened on that date: a parent dying, a partner leaving, an illness contracted. The rest of the family may feel able to express a word of comfort, and to pray with the one who is hurt, and such prayer will be very much appreciated. Those prayers may also give thanks for someone who has died, and bring the family closer together on the special anniversary.

The family I mentioned, who lost three relatives together, took a deliberate decision not to pray at the cemetery, or to lay flowers on the graves each year. Instead they choose someone to whom they give a gift on that day, often a gift of flowers, which they send anonymously. It is a very positive way of showing love to another, as well as to the ones they have lost. The prayers of their home are for the living, as well as to give thanks for the dead.

'Help!'

In all the situations in this and the last two chapters, we should not be too proud to shout out for extra help when we need it. Other families will probably be pleased if we ask them to pray for us. In our home, we are particularly grateful to the families of godparents for their prayers for our children, as well as to a wider family of prayer partners who pray for our work as well as our home.

Conversely, other families will be delighted when they are assured that our family is praying for them. A neighbour's wife died recently, and our card to him told him he was in our prayers. In his letter of thanks he replied, 'Don't stop praying.' We are part of a larger team, and the needs of families around us can focus our prayers, and give impetus to our caring.

Most of all, in every one of these situations, God wants to help us at each step. As the old hymn says, it is a privilege to carry everything to God in prayer. We needlessly carry our own burdens, when he longs to help us in our family life.

PART THREE

Special Times

10

Christmas Day

Even if a family rarely prays together, there are certain times when they can hardly help it! An event will come along when the most natural thing in the world is to turn to God, whether it be through joy, or thanks, or need. When we are happy, we want to praise God. When life gets us down, we feel a need to ask for his help or protection.

This chapter and the three which follow contain lots of ideas for family prayers at special times of the year. No family will do all the things suggested. Equally, the suggestions here are by no means exhaustive. Do-it-yourself planning is the way to go. It can be great fun planning something together which the family then owns. I'm starting with Christmas Day, as my favourite, and a chapter on what we do in our home.

The big day

If ever a day is especially special, it has to be Christmas Day. This is the day to get it right, to make it the best. And we want to make it best for God, too. Because, let's face it, this is the day which is meant to be his, and from which he is all too easily excluded – or at least, side-lined.

The value for the Christian family of putting Jesus Christ at the very centre of the anniversary of his birth cannot be stated too strongly. If we over-trivialise the coming of the Son of God into the world, how will our children ever believe our faith has any real substance? Of all days to remember him, this is the one. Unfortunately, although this is something we all agree with in theory, what to do in practice isn't always so straightforward.

The answer may well be . . . *The Cake.* At least, we have found it to be the answer for our family. The key to Christmas is that it is a birthday. And what do we do for birthdays? We have a party, and a cake with candles, and we sing to and honour the birthday person. So we do it for Jesus on his birthday.

The anticipation starts weeks before, with the making of the cake. We follow the good old tradition of everyone stirring the Christmas pudding and the Christmas cake, so that we all feel part of the action. A few days before the great day dawns, the cake is iced. In big, colourful letters the words appear 'Happy Birthday Jesus'. For some reason I have never fathomed, Ruth, my wife, does ours in bright green – which looks spectacular on the pure white icing. The usual model snowman, fir-trees and so on also find their place. Our Christmas cake is a birthday cake so a candle or two is essential.

On Christmas Eve the table is laid for breakfast. And, in pride of place, there sits the cake, with knife and matches at the ready. This is not going to be a boring old 'Let's get through breakfast quickly so we can get lunch ready' . . . This is going to be a 'WOW'. This breakfast will be a highlight of the entire festive season. Christmas morning never seems to start late. We are into stockings in a big way in our house. Quite a while is spent jumping on the parental bed and opening stockings together.

Breakfast at any other time of the year will be a staggered affair – get it when you arrive. But not this one! The cereals, the toast are but in preparation for The Cake. Yes, we really are going to have Christmas cake for breakfast. It's hard to believe. It may even seem hard to stomach. But it is true!

With cereals and toast on their way into hungry mouths, it is time for the Christmas reading. The choice of reading may depend on the age of those present, but all ages appreciate the wonder of the familiar story of God become a baby. Perhaps with younger children the first few verses of Luke 2 are best. The Christmas story is also told in Matthew 1: 18–25. Or, try the magnificent prophecy about the coming of the Messiah in Isaiah 9:2–7. For an older family, the first fourteen verses of John's Gospel will say it all.

We read with awe. How can you read about 'no room . . . in the inn' without a pang, or that 'we have seen his glory' without wonder? We let it come through, we talk about it. We ask each person what they find best about the reading and we share together the wonder of this special time. We might sing a favourite carol, like 'Away in a manger', or 'Once in royal David's city'.

Then we pray. Perhaps each will pray on this special day. The prayers will mainly be of thanks and praise. But there will also be an element of confession – for so often forgetting the birthday King. And we want to remember before God our extended family, our church family, and those in need.

And now – it's The Cake time! We light the candles, and sing: 'Happy Birthday to you, Happy birthday, dear Jesus!' All blow! Cut the cake, pass it round. Delicious.

Jesus – at the centre of his day: that's where we've placed him. A couple of family presents, and off to church, with the day well under way. Our praise in church is just an extension of that at home. Sitting as a family continues the breakfast birthday party.

And what about the other presents? We open them all through the day. We have a terrific time. Because we brought Jesus in at the beginning, his joy is there all through.

This is now one of the great traditions of our family. We have, with God's help, put Jesus at the centre of our Christmas. We are all glad to have done this, because we want him there. It is a delight, not a duty.

11

Advent to Epiphany

What a splendidly churchy heading for a chapter! I'm going to explore the possibility of making something of either side of Christmas, with a brief further look at what others do on Christmas Day itself. How can we maximise the opportunities for praying at home at this happiest of seasons?

Advent

Advent, the weeks immediately before Christmas, is a very good time for some specific praying as a family. In lots of homes a new candle is lit each Sunday of the four weeks leading up to Christmas Day. It can help the family to look forward prayerfully not only to the anniversary of the first coming of Jesus, but also to his great return as King in the future. Some families make an Advent crown with four candles to light as the centrepiece of the table, and gather around it to read, share and pray. This focuses thoughts on Jesus as the light of the world and can extend into thinking about the world's darkness, and those places which especially need his light.

A Christingle orange has a similar effect to the Advent crown. The idea comes from that part of Europe known as Moravia. An orange has a red ribbon put round it as a reminder of the blood of Jesus given for the whole world.

A candle is stuck in the top to represent Jesus, the Light and the King. Four sticks with bits of fruit on them are the four seasons. These are stuck carefully in so as not to upset the balance of the orange 'world'. As each candle on the crown can give a new idea for prayer, so each symbol of the Christingle gives a new theme for different days in Advent.

We have a lady in our office who was born in Germany, and each Sunday afternoon in Advent her family lights a candle on the crown, sings a couple of carols, prays, and then gets into coffee and cakes in true German style. That's my sort of prayer time! Other families use *The Lion Christmas Book* to read at mealtimes; or have an Advent train with twenty five carriages with presents in – one for each day leading up to Christmas Day; or open Advent calendars or light a daily Advent candle. Somehow we need to restore the spiritual side of this great season, and to help our children escape from a totally godless festival. Advent can be very good for praying together.

Christmas Eve

There are some families who struggle with Christmas Eve, not knowing what to do about Father Christmas, and where God comes in. We're a both/and family. We are great 'stocking' people, but we also enjoy a Christian time together. Priorities are challenged here, because it is very easy to rush round like mad, filling the day with preparations for Christmas Day, and leaving no time for God. A deliberate attempt to find a solution to this is needed. Some relatives of ours carve out a special time for carols, a pop-up book which tells the Christmas story, candles and thanks to God, ensuring that the spiritual side is firmly at the centre of Christmas Eve.

Another family told me how they read through the Christmas story in a picture book and compare it with the Bible's account. They then pray together in anticipation of Christmas. If there are young children in your family, you might like to try *The Christmas Mouse* by Stephanie Jeffs and Jenny Thorpe (Tamarind) or *The First Christmas* (Ladybird). Knowing how full Christmas Day is bound to be, the Eve is a great day to focus on the Christian side of the festival. We sometimes enjoy praying with our wider Christian family on Christmas Eve at a special carol service.

Christmas Day

The previous chapter was very personal! The important thing is for each family to find their own unique way of celebrating, and of centering on Jesus. 'Happy birthday to you' features in many homes, and I know one family where they sing 'ring-a-roses' style round the tree. Lots of families sing carols together, too.

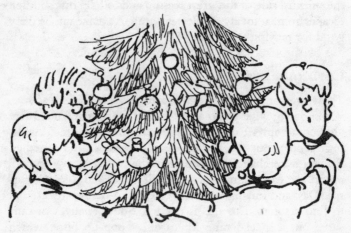

Singing around the Christmas tree . . .

'It's a time to thank God naturally,' one mum told me. In her home, they pray after opening their presents, focusing on God's goodness. Similarly, it may be worth changing grace for a carol before each meal, and praying for those in need when we have so much. One family really goes to town at Christmas lunch: between courses they re-enact the whole Christmas story, using cut-outs for a cow, the donkey, the manger, the star and so on. One of the parents has written out the story to include all the cut-outs (don't make them too big!), and as each is mentioned, it joins a little tableau on the table. Some of the characters are hidden round the house and the children have to find them with the help of clues, encouraged by the sweets hidden with the characters. Lunch must take a long time, but who's rushing?

Epiphany

This day (January 6) marks the coming of the Wise Men and the presentation of their special gifts to the baby Jesus. If the time before Christmas can be used to think about *Christ's coming to us*, as the Light and King, the days after Christmas are a lovely opportunity for us to think, and pray, about *our coming to Christ*. The Wise Men are our examples, as are Anna and Simeon (Luke 2). If you decide to use Epiphany as a focus in your family prayer time, you need to remember not to let the Wise Men feature prominently too soon in the festivities!

Of course, New Year comes during the Christmas season, and can be a very vital time for a family's prayers, looking both at the year past and the year to come. It could be a new beginning for times of prayer.

The whole Christmas season can be a time for the family to know God in a very special way.

12

Go for Easter!

Christmas may have gone secular, but at least most people have an idea what its origins are. Alas for the rest of the Christian calendar! A recent poll shows that a third of people living in Britain do not have a clue what Easter means. This is no time to give up, however. Instead, why not make a point of remembering together at home the different special days of the year's calendar, to help our families think about and enjoy vital elements of what we believe? Almost as soon as Epiphany is over, all sorts of good days come along when prayer can be special.

St Valentine's day

How about Valentine's Day, for example? What a good day for readings and prayers about love! It can be a day to give thanks to God not only for his own love, but for the love we share with each other as well. How special for the children to hear Mum and Dad thank God for each other, as they enjoy the security of a safe, loving home. And, sadly, if parents have separated or divorced, here is an opportunity to thank God for his unfailing love and care for each of us.

Pancake Day

Within a week or so comes Shrove Tuesday or Pancake Day. Making pancakes used to be seen as a way of using up all the sweet, treat foods in the house, before the beginning of Lent, starting the next day on Ash Wednesday. It's a day of celebration and we can, literally, make a meal of it! Why can't God be at the centre of our fun and happiness? The world has a sneaky way of taking a religious festival, and squeezing it till there is no room for Christianity. We can recover what is ours, and in our families thank God for food and laughter and his goodness.

Lent

By contrast, from Ash Wednesday onwards we have the chance to look more closely at the life and teachings of Jesus, especially his sacrifices and sufferings. It is a time for getting our own lives right. Do we ever, as a family, own up to our wrongs and ask God for his Holy Spirit's help? Now could be the time to do this. Holy Week especially can be a journey through the promises Jesus made to his followers in John 12–17, claiming them for each member of the family as we pray. Our family often goes through some of the big events from Palm Sunday to Good Friday in one of the Gospels during Holy Week, and perhaps spends a little longer in prayer about the meaning of this time for us.

Easter

Maundy Thursday is the day before Good Friday and the day of the Last Supper shared by Jesus and his disciples. Like many other families, we try to make this Thursday evening a special time for our family. Following the Jewish Passover tradition, the main ingredient of our evening meal would be roast lamb. Towards the end of the meal, one of the family reads one of the Gospel accounts of the Last Supper. Then someone else reads Paul's version of this in 1 Corinthians 11:23–26. This leads into a simple family communion. A roll, and red wine or blackcurrant drink, are all that is needed. Someone gives thanks for the bread, remembering Jesus' broken body, and each family member takes a piece of the roll. Another person gives thanks for the cup, and we each share the drink, as we recall the blood of Jesus poured out for us. It's a very moving time, and we all feel closer to God, and to each other, as a result. If anyone in the family is *not* a Christian, you could leave out the actual communion together, but still use your evening meal to focus on the story and meaning of the Last Supper – as long as the family feels comfortable with this.

I have friends who invite other families to such a meal, and who follow more closely the Jewish style of the Passover meal. They, for example, have unleavened bread and say the Jewish liturgy. The Matzos (unleavened bread) has to be found by the children after being hidden, and the youngest child asks, 'Why is this night different?' as in a Jewish home.

Some families share communion together in the home on Good Friday itself, either as part of a meal, or as a separate time together. Our Good Friday always includes a short family service, in which we often use the cross on the hot cross buns as a visual focus. We would read one of the crucifixion accounts in a Gospel, and perhaps sing a hymn or song about the cross, followed by prayers of thanks and confession. Then we eat the hot cross buns! Others use Good Friday to build an Easter garden in their own garden, or indoors (on a smaller scale). This garden, with the tomb covered by a stone, is the focus for prayer over the whole Easter holiday. The stone is rolled away after the last child has gone to bed on Saturday night.

For these families, Easter Day begins with the children rushing into the garden to find the tomb empty. They are often joined by their parents in the garden to pray and praise God together at the beginning of this wonderful day. Others begin Easter with many Christian friends on the top of a local hill, welcoming the dawn as one family and singing together.

For others, a grand church service is special for the family. One mum told me of a great cathedral service they always go to on Easter Eve – an all-night service with a candle for each one there, very popular with the children. Easter breakfast is a good time for an Easter morning reading from a Gospel, establishing the truth of the event as well as its joy in the hearts and minds of all in the home. Some families tell me that these days they actually prefer Easter to Christmas, as being a more genuinely Christian festival. They organise an Easter egg hunt (we always do that!), revel in the service at church with its joyful hymns, have another filling of hot cross buns and share a celebratory lunch with friends. It's a good time for some new beginnings in each of our lives, too!

So we can reclaim our Christian heritage, and make each season God's time for our lives. Let's rejoice together in the different days and festivals of the year, letting them teach us more about our God and his life in us.

13

Holy days and holidays

Life is full of wonderful variety. As a year rolls through, every new special event can be turned into an occasion for prayer. Happy days come in all shapes and sizes, and we can let God be the centre and creator of our joy.

Holy days

One of the definitions of 'holy' is 'set apart for God'. Some days come right within that category, others can belong too if we so choose. Easter is hardly over when the festivals of Ascension and Pentecost arrive. What great opportunities they offer for praying in the family. Those dramatic readings at the end of Matthew (28:16–20), Mark (16:15–20) and the beginning of Acts (1:1–11), can be focal points for talking together, as well as praying. This is the time of year for agreeing with the man who said, 'My ambition is to go to heaven, and to take as many people with me as I can.'

Children and adults alike will value the chance of asking the big questions about Jesus as Lord of heaven, and about the Holy Spirit. At Pentecost we can ask God to help us understand more about his Spirit, and about the gifts and fruit he brings. We can read together extracts from Acts 2 (the coming of the Holy Spirit), 1 Corinthians 12 (the gifts) and Galatians 5:22–23 (the fruit). Pictures of fire and wind might be helpful, and I have found the various segments in an orange to be a good visual aid of several parts of one fruit to explain Galatians 5:22–23. With a little thought and creativity, prayers take on an extra dynamic.

This is also the time of year when our family has its birthdays, and these can be very special opportunities for prayer, as we thank God for all the birthday person means to us, and as we bless them for all the next year will mean in their life. Prayer is a great way of affirming a person, and letting them know how precious they are to God, and to us. Those families who rarely pray together can make a 'special' day of a birthday, even if it is done during an extended grace, with thanks and blessings for the person as well as the meal. Similarly, a wedding anniversary is a time for praise, and re-dedication by the family of the marriage. Ruth and I went to a terrific twenty-fifth anniversary celebration of one marriage, where the whole family prayed with their guests, and sang God's praises as a group in front of us. It was quite moving, and a challenge for everyone there, as well as a testimony to how God had kept and led that couple through all their time together.

A large part of family life with children inevitably surrounds going to school, and I know homes where they look out for opportunities to make a feature of praying for something which is happening in school. A couple of days away with the school may be a child's first absence from parents, and can be an opportunity for prayers of blessing and protection. One dad told me how he cooks a special meal at the end of a term, and makes that day a chance for thanksgiving – even if the school report is not all it might have been. (Perhaps he remembers what his own were like!) Some families use the start of an academic year as a time for special prayers, especially if the children are going to a different school, or will have a new teacher, or different classmates. And during the school year the joys and pains are for God to share, and the hurts caused by bullying, loneliness, or inability to cope, occasions to pray with children 'deliver us from evil'.

Autumn brings harvest, with its glory, colour and richness. What a good time for praise! It also brings Hallowe'en, which more and more families use as an opportunity to come against evil in Jesus' name. It can be difficult to know how to respond to the various activities planned for this day. We do not want to spoil our children's fun, or make them seem like kill-joys to their friends. Neither do we want to emphasise the more sinister aspects of Hallowe'en. Some Christian families get together for an alternative celebration with games, singing and prayers.

So any special day can become an occasion for prayer. I love the way a mum told me how, when she and her family moved house recently, they all went into every empty room, praying for it to be filled with love. This was after sitting in the hall of their old home to thank God for all the happiness they had known there. Another mum told me how she had gone back to work after an absence of some years as she had cared for small children. The whole family, now growing up, had gathered round and prayed for her as she took this big step. Happiness and adventure are for God to share, and bless!

Holidays

'Holy days' are still around, but the words have changed into 'holidays'. The two can still be the same, with no difficulty at all. Holidays offer a unique opportunity for family togetherness, and especially for coming closer to God as the members come closer to each other – a time for re-creation and recreation.

Some families choose to go on holidays which are specifically Christian. 'We made a conscious decision to have a Christian holiday as a family,' one couple told me. 'Christian activities are laid on, we meet with other Christian families, and we can pray and sing and worship together.' The opportunities for such a holiday are many, whether it be to a camp or houseparty, an event like Spring Harvest or the Keswick Convention, or a trip abroad run by a Christian organisation. The important thing is for the family to agree that this is what each member really wants to do. When home time comes, the family's prayer life will probably have benefited no end, to say nothing of the good times praying together when away.

Some families go to the opposite extreme, and their prayer life falls apart on holiday as routines disappear. This may not be as bad as it seems, and I know one family who see their fellowship together on holiday as being a form of prayer in itself, and their lack of formal praying gives prayer back at home a new impetus. The last thing prayer should do is make us feel guilty when we don't get it quite right! In fact, those families I spoke with who 'carry on as usual' with their normal family prayers routine whilst on holiday were the ones who seemed least satisfied with their way of doing things.

Holidays should be times for variety, for doing different and new things, for adventure, even in prayer. For example, some families only sing together on holiday. A long car journey can be relieved with good praise tapes. Every family will have their own favourites. Why not sing along? Quite a lot of family worship can happen going round the M25! One family told me that they begin each day on holiday with the prayer, 'Lord, give us something free to do today that's really great.' A walk or an outing can be transformed by bringing God into it. Our enjoyment of God's creation and conversation about it can lead into praise to our Maker as we walk and talk together.

And what about worship on holidays? This is an opportunity to sample a different style of church, perhaps, or meet with new Christians. But many families, ours included, do their own thing. 'We have a family service, sitting up on the Downs,' one family told me. Singing, praying, reading, sharing, have an added spice when done in the countryside, or by the seashore. Especially when in another country with

101

no service in English nearby (though look out for the many organised by Intercon), the family might come to look forward to their own family 'do-it-yourself' service.

One of the children might 'do the talk'. It's probably best to choose a theme in advance, perhaps fitting the place where you're staying (the sea, the hills, the rain, other races, for example). Ask for volunteers from the family to do different things on the chosen topic. A prayer from one, a song from another, a reading from a third, and a 'thought for the day', and you have your service. If there is another Christian family nearby, why not join together with them?

Perhaps some of the family might find it embarrassing to have a family service outside with others around. One mum told me that one of her children said that she could not cope with people watching them worship on their French camp site. The other child piped up, 'Why should we be embarrassed? People sit naked on the beach, and they're not shy!' As long as it is enjoyable, not too long, and real, a holiday family service can be one of the most lovely things ever shared.

I'm glad our holidays are times for being together. And I'm particularly glad that we can get together with God, even if it's only for Sunday worship. It's worth doing!

14

Hard times

The turning years bring times of great happiness, as we have just seen. But how does the Christian family win through when one or more of its members is struggling? In this chapter and the next we'll take a look at some of those hard times we all go through.

The pressure of exams

Our family has reached that dreadful stage when exams matter. The odd day or two preparing for a school test has stretched to months of getting ready for exams which can affect a whole future. How can we help our children in praying during this traumatic time?

When I sat my first big exams my mother did a wonderful thing. On the morning of the first exam, while I was in the bathroom she left a letter on my bedroom table. In it she had written that she wished me well and assured me of her prayers during every paper I sat. Then she quoted Isaiah 26:3:

> You will keep in perfect peace him whose mind is steadfast, because he trusts in you.

Years later I can still feel the sense of peace which this note and its promise brought. When our children have faced their biggest hurdles, we have written similarly to them.

I know of other parents, too, who tell me how they look for verses of encouragement for their children at times of exams, or other difficulties or crises, such as the painful breakdown of a relationship. Many families make such times an opportunity for very special prayer, including asking for God's calm in the heart and mind of the child concerned. We can pray for nervousness to be minimal, and for our child to be able to recall what they have learnt. I was reminded by one dad how important it is to assure a child that God's love doesn't depend on passing or failing an exam, and neither does the parents'. God will help children to do their best.

On the other hand, it doesn't help to let a child believe that God is a sort of insurance policy person, who will enable them to pass the exam without working for it. In praying with our children about their exams, we try to help them picture themselves as co-workers. God is not a 'crutch', but neither is he disinterested: he cares for us, and we must care enough to work for him. Prayer for exams needs to start long before the dreaded day itself, as the family prays for good days of learning at school, and the ability to get down to effective homework and study.

When the day of the first exam dawns, we can say to the child, 'O.K. you've done your bit, now we can give the whole thing to God.' Children value enormously hearing the whole family pray for them before a test or exam, or a big sporting fixture. Some families extend this with everyone gathering round the examinee to lay hands on them, so the prayer is felt as well as heard.

After each exam, I have a policy of not asking how it went, but of saying instead, 'How are you? How do you feel in yourself?' I want my children to know that my greatest concern is for their well-being, not their success or otherwise. Of course we care about the results, and a good mark deserves praise, whatever the child feels. One mum's first encounter with her young daughter's success was when the

child ran up with the news, 'Mummy, I've got an extinction!'
The results are a time for talking to God and trusting him
with the future, even if the results are apparently a disaster!

This attitude of prayer at exam time can continue. And as
children go on to further education, they know the family
will still gather to pray for them in their absence.

The pain of parting

The problem for some homes is that family life is too good!
As someone leaves, heading out to their own future,
excitement is tinged with the sadness of parting. When our
eldest son left home for college, I felt bereaved. At our family
prayer time that day, Ruth, my wife, had to do the praying:
I was too choked up to cope! I laid hands on him as we sent
him off with God's blessing, and with all our love. Each time
he comes home, he receives a special send-off in prayer
when he returns to college. Lots of families follow a similar
pattern, and it helps both the one going and those staying
to cope with the parting, and to be glad that God is at the
centre of this important moment.

One family who has had several children leave home at
different times told me how they either pray at breakfast, or
as the child is going out of the door. They all gather round,
lay their hands on him or her, and commit them to the
Lord's protection, as a sort of mini-commissioning. Another
family shared how they all stand in a circle at this moment
of parting, while, on the pavement or on a station platform,
Dad commends the whole family to God.

If the family is going with the one who is leaving to their
new 'home', it may be best to pray with them there. The
leaver then knows that his or her strange new home has been
offered to God by the family, and that their prayers remain
after they have left.

Similarly, the assurance of continuing prayers is a great
comfort, as well as an encouragement, for the absentee. Our
son knows he is prayed for by all of us together at about

8.20am each day, and we have his timetable on our kitchen notice-board to help us be as specific as possible. He will sometimes ask in a letter, or on the phone, for a particular situation to be prayed about. Some families admit that they pray more earnestly for a child when he is away from home than when he is present!

I asked my son about our praying for him, and he said he felt better able to live as a Christian because of this support, and the strength God gave as a result. We have been thrilled to see the way his life with Christ has blossomed, and I am delighted when he feels able to mention a need for us to bring to God. His brothers pray for the Christian Union he leads and so identify with his stand. As an evangelist, I also am glad that I have a family at home praying for me when I am away preaching, and their support in this way lifts my spirits when the going gets tough.

When someone is a great distance away from home, prayer may be the only lifeline which holds a family together. At times like this, a family can prove that prayer really does work, especially if others are on hand to share in the praying. One of my colleagues at work promised that his family would pray for the daughter of another family as she went off to Cairo in 1992 to work with a missionary society. Early in 1993, Cairo was struck by a massive earthquake, which killed many. The concerned family in England were strengthened by their own prayers, and those of my colleague's family. Telephoning was impossible, but my colleague prayed for news of the girl's safety that evening, and again when he woke at 7.30am the next day. Her father had been trying to get through to her on the phone from 5am that morning. He made contact with his shaken but unharmed daughter at – yes – 7.30am, whilst my colleague had been praying.

As we face up to the inevitable moving on of our family members, it can be a time for strengthening our ties in prayer. Our God binds us together, and although the distance of the miles may cause heartache, our spirits are at one through his Holy Spirit.

Concerns near and far

But what if the exams produce a 'fail', or the leaving home is unhappy? And what of our other heartfelt concerns? There are times which prove very hard indeed, when we need more than ever to cry out to God as we pray together. A child, or a parent, may not get a job, or find themselves out of work. Now is the time to stand together, united in prayer, believing in a God who loves and cares for each of us. Now is the time to hold on to God. This must also be the way if someone leaves home under a cloud, or drifts away, or goes to a less than satisfactory situation. We need to remember that God loves our children even more than we do, and his love and protection will go with them.

Similarly, when our children become all-but impossible to cope with, through their rebellion or deliberate, protracted disobedience, we can turn even more in prayer to a God who knows those children better than we do. He knows the way through, and our prayers may be the most important thing for those children at such a time. If, on reflection, we realise some of the blame must be at our own door, we may have to confess our failure openly, asking for God's forgiveness – which may well help the children who hear our prayer. Perhaps we will save our most heart-broken prayers for private, so as not to disturb unduly those other family members who are coping well.

In all these hard situations, I do believe we need to be honest in our praying. A family will quickly see through trite words spoken to God. He wants us to share our heart concerns with him, however tough the situation. The same applies when the outside world's problems cause us grief. A bad incident in the day's news is surely worthy of an honest prayer of concern, and even for tears over the brokenness of mankind. Speaking of brokenness, it is time to look at a very major aspect of praying together as a family – when illness strikes. That is the subject of the next chapter.

15

Illness and healing

If a family never prays at any other time, they may well be driven to it when illness strikes. For every family which does pray, the health and well-being of its members, and those close to it, will be a regular topic. Our encouragement for this comes from Jesus himself, whose concern to heal family members is seen throughout his ministry: Peter's mother-in-law (Mark 1:31), Jairus' daughter (Luke 8:54–55), the foreign lady's child (Mark 7:29) and Lazarus (John 11:43–44). All these knew about the healing power of Jesus in his compassionate response to a family's request.

'Daddy, poorly eye, Amen.'

Illness is the classic case of need generating prayer. One two year old's first prayer, her dad told me, was when she put her hand on his face and said, 'Daddy, poorly eye, Amen.' Whenever anyone is ill in the family, others in the family and those close to them will want to pray for their healing. For many homes, illness is the major theme in praying, as prayer and medicine get doled out together! It is almost instinctive to hold a sick child, touching the place of illness as you pray. For any Christian family, and many a non-Christian one, it is instinctive to want to pray for a family member who is unwell as soon as a problem arises. How can we get this right, so both we and our children know God is answering these heartfelt prayers?

Problems

Some people are embarrassed by illness, and have a real struggle knowing what to pray for. What if the prayers don't 'work'? A good friend of mine had an uncle who was ill. Every day the family prayed, 'Lord, please bless Uncle Jim, and help him to get better.' After three weeks, he died. Not long afterwards, a young man in their church fell ill, so every day the family prayed, 'Lord, please bless Mark, and help him to get better.' Several days into these prayers, the four year old asked, 'Is Mark going to die now?'! The mother did not tell me how she followed that! We are into tricky theology here. God does not always answer our prayers in the way we want. This is not only a mystery, but an important lesson for life, and one which will need a simple, honest and caring explanation when questions are asked by a small child.

The opposite result is not any easier to handle: immediate 'success' will need to be carefully explained too. A Sunday group teacher was not present one Sunday. She had gone into hospital after a lump in her breast had been discovered. It was explained to the children that this teacher was in hospital, and they were asked to pray for her to get better. Fifteen minutes later she walked in! The lump had receded.

The children and their leader were astounded, and they thanked God for answering their prayers. The problem was how not to give the impression that a sort of magic wand could be waved to cure all ills.

The third difficulty is one we have had to face in our own family: to accept that we really are in God's hands in this world. We like to be in control, even in praying. Illness reminds us that we're dependent on God. When our second son was very small he had the measles, which progressed to pneumonia and then suspected meningitis. I well remember my prayer, as the nurse gave him the injection which could save his life: 'Lord, if you take him, he's yours; and if you give him back, he's yours.' It was a moment of absolute trust: there was nothing else I could do. At that moment I knew God's arms were around us, and he did recover. But I also recall praying exactly those words when my brother lay dying after a terrible accident as a missionary in Uganda – and he died.

This whole subject is a very tough one, and tests our faith in a loving God more than almost anything else. That is why we need to

Be careful!

When someone is ill, it may be good to pray with each child individually, enabling hard questions to be asked and answered, as well as for the prayer to be at its most intimate. That may be right even if the sick person is not a child, but a parent who is in hospital, for example. We have prayed individually with our children if they were ill in the night, or if they were disturbed by bad dreams, or frightened. It is a precious moment when a child comes and says 'Daddy, please pray for me,' and we can hold him and pray for his need at once.

Whether with one person, or the whole family, there does need to be a relaxed atmosphere when praying for healing, with no great song and dance. If it feels right to lay hands on a child who is ill, I find it better to do it naturally by being alongside them, rather than to say over-seriously, 'I'm going to lay hands on you now.' Holding a child is something they expect, and touching the place of pain will make them feel our care, as well as God's, without our spelling out the deeper significance of 'the laying on of hands'. That's what I mean by being careful and sensitive.

Often it is not the illness itself, but a particular fear within the context of the illness which causes concern to a child, and which we need to pray about. If we can step back and work this out carefully, we may avoid all sorts of difficulties. One seven year old was in hospital with serious stomach problems. His mum was careful enough to realise that the crisis he faced was not his stomach, but his fear of hospitals and needles. Because of this, she made sure she prayed with him when his drip was changed and when the doctors came round, holding his hand to reassure him. When he asked why he was not healed, his mum was honest enough to answer 'I don't know,' and he was satisfied with that. As I write, he is still not fully well.

If we feel that specific prayer for healing is needed, then I take a leaf out of one family's book, whose young son was very ill. They asked some friends to come round and pray over him, but waited until he was sound asleep before they gathered round his bed. In this way he was not overwhelmed by a group of non-family adults, nor was he made to feel he was in extra-serious need of prayer. A little thought and care can work wonders – and he did improve significantly as a result.

Prayer for healing

The intimacy of a family is an ideal situation for trusting each other in praying for a true and lasting healing for the one who is ill. Whether none, or one, or all lay hands on the sick member is up to the individual family's style, and time and circumstances may dictate a different approach on certain occasions. We can pray for grace and peace to cope with the illness as well as specific healing. I am struck by the way Jesus' aim was to make people 'whole', so that they were made completely well, not just in their bodies. There is no harm in our telling Jesus how we would like to feel. I am convinced we can expect an answer.

Clearly, we are going to pray about specific ills to be put right: the 'flu, the measles, pneumonia, having a hard time breathing, aches and pains, bumps and cuts, gunged-up eyes, asthma – the more families I met, the longer grew the list of things people bring to God in prayer! And there need be no end to this list, because God does care for us whatever the situation, and says of himself:

I am the Lord who heals you (Exodus 15:26).

Nor should this sort of prayer be the exclusive prerogative of adults. Families tell me how children pray for their parents, as well as vice versa. If Mum or Dad is lying in bed, the children are in the driving seat! How lovely for them to lay hands on a sick adult and pray for healing. It can enrich the relationship, especially if the parent is gracious and humble enough to let it happen. Similarly, if a parent is facing an operation, it is a great source of strength if the family can gather round at breakfast before Mum or Dad leaves. If a parent or child has a continuing illness, the family may want to pray on for months and even years, encouraging the sick person not to give up, but to trust God for his right timing.

Always our praying for specific healing should claim the authority of the name of Jesus, as the one who is mighty to save and heal.

Outside help

Illness is not the place for pride, and a wise family will ask others for their support in prayer when things are badly wrong. This may mean, as James 5 urges, the sending for the leaders of the church to pray with and for the sick. Of course, this is likely to go alongside sending for the doctor! If the person who is ill is able to get to church, there may be an opportunity for prayer in the context of the service, or the church may have a prayer chain which can be contacted so several will pray for the situation.

Recently my young niece Esther had a serious sight problem, and my sister and her husband were told that there was a good chance that she would lose all vision in one eye. Sue and Derek read what the Bible had to say about healing and about anointing the sick person with oil and they felt it was right to ask for a service of healing, after talking with their minister. When they knew the time of the service they wrote to a number of friends, and phoned others, asking them to pray at the specific time when the minister would be leading the service. So Esther would not be overwhelmed, they invited less than ten people to join them at the church, and only told her what was going to happen the day before the event.

Five minutes before they were due to leave, Esther, in floods of tears, decided she did not want to go. Her reason was quite understandable. She thought the oil would run down her face and be very embarrassing. (She had thoughts of a huge bottle of cooking oil!). The minister showed her his phial of oil, and she felt better about it. Sue and Derek took her forward in the church, and several, including Derek, prayed for her before the eye was anointed with oil. There have been three results: Esther was not immediately healed; she did accept an eye-patch with God-given patience; and over a relatively short length of time the eye has improved dramatically, with her vision getting better to the surprise of the specialists. Sue and Derek are as delighted as Esther, though they say that, if they did it again, they would ask Esther's permission from the beginning.

Prayers for people . . . and pets

It is not only our families that get ill: others do, too! There is a real ministry a family can share in praying for others. But what about the animal kingdom? Should we pray for our pets? I know one dad who had real problems with praying for the rabbit, though another had no difficulty praying for the dog when it had an operation! Was this why, in the one case the rabbit died, while the dog got better?! It is adults who struggle with such questions, not children. One mum confessed that she did not know whether to pray for the guinea-pig with pneumonia, and its weekly injections, as the children wanted. When she hesitated about praying, the children phoned Granny, who said it was no problem, and they prayed right then on the phone. The guinea-pig was better within three days. . . .

. . . the dog got better . . .

If we can pray about our pets' problems, we will certainly want to pray for our wider family members, friends and neighbours in their illnesses. Nearly every family prayer time will include one sick person or another. We will feel we are onto something important when praying together for a big problem, such as when a person close to us appears to be dying. Part of being in a wider church family is bearing others' burdens. The need may demand an immediate crisis prayer gathering of the family members around at the time, before we jump in the car to see Granny who has just been rushed to hospital, or when something urgent comes down the church prayer chain.

The family might stop to pray while an operation is taking place or, as we did with Esther and her service, pray with others at a certain time when we unite across the miles. Similarly, after visiting a sick person, it might be good to sit and pray together in the car before driving home. Sometimes we find that someone who is sick will only trust one particular person to pray for them. I heard of one five year old whose friend had trapped his finger at school. His Christian parents had tried to pray with him, but he wouldn't let them. The little girl insisted that she should be taken to visit her friend. When she arrived he was willing for her, and only her, to see his hand and pray for it, and him.

If ever there is a place for prayer in the family, it is for the health and wholeness of the members of that family and those close to them. God the Healer is waiting, and wanting to answer.

16

The family in church

Just as an individual is part of a family, so our families are part of the wider family of God's church. That is where we should be, joining with his people:

> Let us not give up meeting together . . . but let us encourage one another (Hebrews 10:25).

Together in church

Most Christian families want to be part of a local church family and aim to make regular attendance at a service an automatic weekly event. Getting everyone ready to go in time can be a real pressure, and the service might prove to be a headache sometimes, with the strain of keeping junior abnormally quiet. Even so – it *is* worth it!

By making a habit of regularly meeting with other Christians for a service, we are not only helping our children see the vital place of corporate worship, but we are helping them form positive values. From their regular meeting with the wider Christian family, they learn that their family's beliefs are not odd ideas held in opposition to the rest of the world, but that we share with others a common faith which is right, and worth having. Nor is this a one way process, for our family will have much to offer the local church in the help we can give, the encouragement we can share and the friendship we can offer, especially to the lonely and alone. With our enthusiasm, grown in the prayer life of the home, we may be able to preach, teach, run the crèche, work the sound system, play in the music group, boost the numbers in the youth activities, swell the congregation . . . the opportunities are enormous.

And what a good feeling it is to be sitting together, worshipping alongside each other and taking part in the service in one way or another. This sense of mutual encouragement will move our Christian lives forward significantly. The highlight of a parent's week may be the moment the little one comes back in from her Sunday group to show off proudly what has been made, and to stand on the seat singing 'Bosanna to the King'! These are special moments. Nor does family worship help only Christians – it is a huge support for those who have not yet come to faith, especially adults. If Mum, or Dad, or another relative, is groping towards becoming a Christian, they will feel safe sitting alongside a non-critical family, and so be helped, much more so than if they were isolated, to move forward positively.

Some churches occasionally have a time for individual families to share together as a family during the service. Often this is done during a communion service, where the family will receive the bread and the cup as one unit, and this can be a source of great strength, though it may be difficult for lone Christians. It is certainly a good way of re-uniting a family which has separated at the door of the church because of their different 'jobs' during the service time. And it gives a very special time for prayer together in the context of the church, rather than the home. The minister might also feel able to bless the family units, especially if there is a hurt, or burden, or need. Another way families often contribute as a unit to the wider church family is by leading the prayers during a service. Planning for this can bring much stimulation to the family's prayer times at home.

Other churches have times of prayer for special needs, including healing, with friends gathering round to pray, and perhaps the laying on of hands. It can be a most precious moment when a parent finds his own child praying for him in this way though, if it is the child who is ill, the parent may hold back to respect her privacy. I personally find great strength from my children's support when I am preaching, and need no more encouragement than for one of them to say afterwards, 'Good sermon, Dad!' An encouraging nod from a partner can work wonders, too! When one of the family is active in church life, the rest can play a vital role in support and prayer while they are 'up front'.

Separate in church

Often we are *not* together in church, at least, not physically. For very many active Christian families, that is invariably the case. We would like to sit together, and to feel we are worshipping together, but we can't always. One is involved in the music group, another is on duty welcoming people and the children are in their Sunday groups. It is a hard choice between our desire to be together as a nuclear family and the opportunities to worship, pray, serve and learn, separately within the context of the wider church family. A child may find it difficult to go off to a group for his particular age group, and yet gain much from doing so, including learning how to be an independent Christian, with his family nearby. If the youth section meets in such a way that they do not join in the church service at all, and yet have a brilliant time by themselves, parents are bound to feel that dilemma keenly but can support the youth leaders thankfully in prayer. It will not be nearly as hard, in any case, as for those families who separate at home, with some going to church and some not.

Some families actually feel that church is *not* the place to be together, and that each should sit with their contemporaries and personal friends, praying and being with them. A family may arrive at the church door, and only meet up again at that door when it is time to go home, and yet feel that is very good. One heads with musical instrument to the front, another is with the baby ready to go to the crèche, a parent is teaching a class, and so on. Each will pray, but not with their nuclear family. The church becomes the family and through this experience the family's spiritual life is greatly enhanced.

Our own 'church'

When I was little, my dad would go out to church in the evening, leaving Mum and us children at home. Whilst he was out we loved to make up our own evening service, with dressing gowns for robes, a table for a pulpit, and even a collection plate! In we would process, with Mum being the entire congregation. It was where we first learned to do something in the context of the church. I was delighted to meet one family which does this today: the children decide a theme for the service, read from the Bible, learn a memory verse, choose the hymns, take up an offering – and all for Mum!

Once in a while the church can come to us, and revitalise our family praying. As families, our churches are for us to give to and receive from, and so grow closer to God.

PART FOUR

Family Prayers

17

Good prayers

What is a 'good' prayer?

When is a prayer a good prayer? How can we help our families feel that they are getting it right? I have talked with a lot of families, and family members, to discover the answers, and certain words kept cropping up in their replies.

The word used by most people was 'honesty'.

'What's a good prayer?' I asked.

'You mean it,' a mum replied. 'Never mind the language, length or phrases – you must mean what you're saying.'

'Say it how it is,' said one dad, 'This is me, recognising how I feel, and being honest with God, recognising who he is.'

That must be right: to be honest, and know that Jesus accepts us as we are. If we don't know what to say, then why not say so? What an encouragement to the whole family when they hear a parent telling God the truth.

Close on the heels of honesty came 'simplicity'. I am a great one for KISS (Keep It Simple, Stupid), and believe a childlike (not childish) faith is the secret of Christian living. Being natural with God, trusting him to hear and answer, communicating in such a way that God hears through our confusion to the real cry of our hearts, and avoiding flowery language: our children will appreciate these as much as God!

Everyone can identify with a straightforward approach, which is spontaneous and from the heart, and even sometimes has a little humour. It links with that other vital word, 'reality', as we aim not to impress the listeners, but to be real with God. I heard of a boy who prayed, 'Lord, you know I can't be good all the time, but help me to be good some of the time'! Our family prayer times are *us* meeting God as we are, and trusting him to be our God and Father. When one of our sons went in to hospital, a younger friend of his prayed, during his family prayers, 'Father God, please look after him when he has his operation, and please keep him company.' That is being real!

Reality will help 'spontaneity'. We can come to God with immediate prayers as families, without the need to wait for a special event like church on Sunday, and pray about what is happening here and now. Many families I spoke with thought that good prayers are often short prayers! I was glad, too, that many spoke about 'thankfulness'. It's something we can easily forget, as we go straight into a shopping-list of needs. It is easy to forget God's loving care.

If a family gets into a rut in its praying, there are one or two guidelines some people use to help their prayers be good and relevant. An acrostic on PRAY Praise, Repent, Ask, You can give a simple structure, as can ACTS Adoration, Confession, Thanksgiving, Supplication. The latter is a bit tricky in its vocabulary, especially for younger ones. FAT sounds fun (Forgive, Ask, Thanks). I know some who use the fingers of the hand: the thumb is for praise, the forefinger for thanks, the biggest for confession, the ring finger is our prayers for others, ending with the smallest finger to pray for ourselves. One family told me that they based their prayers on 'thank you' and 'help', and I think that is what ours boil down to as well.

In our family, we try to incorporate all these ideas into the basic question, 'What would we like to pray about today?' As we go round each person for their answer, our joys, sorrows, hopes and fears for the immediate past and future come to the surface.

How about a 'food' prayer?

As I said earlier in the book, a great way to start praying together as a family is to say a grace at mealtimes. Our own family's grace must be the most ordinary in the world: 'Lord Jesus, thank you for our lovely breakfast, Amen.' It is only slightly better than not saying one at all! Nor do we hold hands, as some do – but then we *are* all boys except Mum!

I was brought up with the formality of, 'For what we are about to receive, may the Lord make us truly thankful,' which needs lots of emphasis to stop it being mere words. Others, too, use a grace they have heard elsewhere:

> Bless this food, and make us good.

> Or: Let us eat simply so others may simply eat.

> Or: For every cup and plateful,
> Lord, make us truly grateful.

Many families make up their own grace. Something like this may be said: 'Thank you Lord for the food. We really like Sunday lunch. We think Mum's cooking is great, and thank you that Grandma's here.' Short and sweet is the order of the day, or the food gets cold. If a child prays a 'thank you' for the dog, Dad may have to add 'and breakfast'! I was warned, by one family, of the danger of making a meal of the grace itself, so the real meal was ruined. Mentioning every last item on the menu, those who are starving, and so on, may not find favour with the hungry round the table! We can be grateful in a general way for the pepper, the potatoes and the bananas and tactfully leave out the word 'lovely' if the meal looks as if it might be a disaster! However, a brief reference to the needy may be appropriate, as may a mention of those sharing with us as guests.

Songs are a popular alternative to a spoken grace in some families. A lively rendering of, 'For health and strength and daily food we give you thanks O Lord, Amen' is great. One family I know even make it a six part round! Many go for, 'Thank you Lord for this nice food, right where we are', or 'for this nice tea'. Others sing a doxology, 'Praise God from whom all blessings flow'. Our family unites in the harvest chorus, 'All good gifts around us, are sent from heaven above' – usually when we have visitors! Another family I know go to town with:

> Thank you for the world so sweet, hum hum,
> Thank you for the food we eat, yum yum,
> Thank you for the birds that sing a ling a ling,
> Thank you Lord, for everything. Amen.

When in doubt, be careful. Asked to say grace at Sunday lunch with special guests present, the little boy was nonplussed. His mother suggested he should say what Daddy had said at breakfast, and – so the story goes – he did: 'O God, we've got those dreadful people coming to lunch; give me strength'!

He repeated what his Dad had said at breakfast . . .

A blessing

On several occasions I have mentioned blessings as a particular sort of family prayer, and they can be very special. Bed-time is a natural moment for blessing a child, even if asleep. The child may see the action as a cuddle, while the parent sees it as a way of asking for God's blessing on that child. If a child in our family was ill, or in need, I would pray for God to bless them as they slept, often putting a hand lightly on their head.

Similarly, 'The Lord bless you', accompanied by a hug, may seem right as someone leaves home in the morning.

Blessings do not have to be given in only one direction. Children can do the same for their parents.

One father said: 'Many times I go into my children's bedroom when they are asleep, and pray for God to have his hand on them, with his keeping power, his wisdom and protection, and that he will make them his disciples. I lay my hands on them, though they don't know. If my prayers can help keep them, I never want in the future to say I wish I had prayed more.'

As the old Irish farewell blessing puts it:

May the road rise to meet you,
May the wind be always at your back.
May the sun shine upon your face,
The rains fall soft upon your fields.
And, until we meet again,
May God hold you in the palm of his hand.

Which brings us to . . .

A favourite prayer

I know that most praying in the home and the family will be extemporary, both by parents and children. Occasionally a family might share in what we call 'The Lord's Prayer' and some have other favourite prayers which they enjoy using.

125

Among these would be collects from the services of Morning and Evening Prayer in the Alternative Service Book such as:

> Almighty and everlasting Father, we thank you that you have brought us safely to the beginning of this day. Keep us from falling into sin or running into danger; order us in all our doings; and guide us to do always what is right in your eyes; through Jesus Christ our Lord.

And the beautiful evening prayer:

> Lighten our darkness, Lord, we pray; and in your mercy defend us from all perils and dangers of this night; for the love of your only Son, our Saviour Jesus Christ.

A very old prayer may be popular in a family, such as a version of Mary's song (Luke 1:46–55); or the classic prayer of Ignatius Loyola:

> Teach us, good Lord, to serve thee as thou deservest, to give and not to count the cost, to fight and not to heed the wounds, to toil and not to seek for rest, to labour and not to ask for any reward, save that of knowing that we do thy will, through Jesus Christ our Lord.

Living in Coventry, I know families who like the Coventry Litany of Reconciliation from our Cathedral, which includes lines like: 'The greed which exploits the work of human hands and lays waste the earth'; 'The lust which dishonours the bodies of men, women and children'; and 'The pride which leads us to trust in ourselves and not in God', each line being followed by, 'Father, forgive.'

No family should be without the incomparable *Lion Book of Children's Prayers*. Like many other families, we have been bringing up our children on such gems as:

For sausages, baked beans and crisps
For papers full of fish and chips
For ice cream full of chocolate bits
Thanks, God.
For furry caterpillars to keep
For woodlice with their tickly feet
For crabs we catch with bits of meat
Thanks, God.
For bicycles and roller skates
For playing football with my mates
For times when I can stay up late
Thanks, God.

Our prayer

Now it's time to do it. Let's get on, and let's never stop our prayers as families, so that all the children may say, 'Amen'.

Robert Louis Stevenson wrote some great books, including *Treasure Island*. But he got it absolutely right for me when he wrote the following prayer, which is for my home:

> Lord, behold our family here assembled. We thank you for this place in which we dwell; for the love that unites us, for the peace accorded us this day, for the hope with which we expect the morrow, for the health, the work, the food and the bright skies that make our lives delightful; for our friends in all parts of the earth. Give us courage and gaiety and the quiet mind. Bless us, if it may be, in all our innocent endeavours. And if it may not, give us strength to encounter that which is to come, that we may be brave in peril, constant in tribulation, temperate in wrath, and in all changes of fortune and down to the gates of death, loyal and loving to one another. As the clay to the potter, as the windmill to the wind, as the children to their father, we beseech you of this help and mercy, for Christ's sake.

PS A bit more help

Prayers for families

The Lion Book of Children's Prayers, Lion.
Prayers for Children, Juliet Harmer, Scripture Union.
Prayers for Families, Benjamin Jenks, Hodder and Stoughton.
Prayers for all the Family, Michael Botting, Kingsway.
Bill Hogg's Most Excellent Guide to Praying, Kingsway.

Praying for others

Tearaways, On Target from TEAR Fund (100 Church Road, Teddington, Middlesex TW11 8QE). Regular publications aimed at informing and motivating children (and their families) to pray about current needs in the Third World.
Operation Mobilisation produce a world prayer map (The Quinta, Weston Rhyn, Oswestry, Shropshire SY10 7LT).
CARE produce a free quarterly prayer guide (CARE, 53 Romney Street, London SW1P 8RF).

Help with Bible reading

Quest (7s–11s), *One to One* (10s–13s), *Alive to God* (adult), *Daily Bread* (adult) from Scripture Union.
Early Days with Jesus, TOPZ from CWR.

Bibles for family prayer

The Ladybird Bible Story Book, SU.
The Lion Children's Bible, Lion.
The Beginner's Bible, Kingsway.
NIV Children's Edition, Hodder & Stoughton.

Christmas and Easter

The Christmas Mouse, Stephanie Jeffs and Jenny Thorne, SU.
The First Christmas, Ladybird.
A King is Born, Patricia St John, SU.
The Lion Christmas Book, Lion.

Other ideas for family times

Family Fusion, Paul T. Johnson, SU.
Once a Week Family Time, Ishmael, Kingsway.
Family Pilgrim's Progress, retold by Jean Watson, SU.